THE BEST GUESS

ASKING LIFE'S BIG QUESTIONS IN AN AGE OF UNLIMITED ANSWERS

SAM WITTKE

WESTBOW
P R E S S®
A DIVISION OF THOMAS NELSON
& ZONDERVAN

WestBow Press books may be ordered through booksellers or by contacting:

WestBow Press
A Division of Thomas Nelson & Zondervan
1663 Liberty Drive
Bloomington, IN 47403
www.westbowpress.com
844-714-3454

ISBN: 978-1-6642-2725-5 (sc)
ISBN: 978-1-6642-2726-2 (hc)
ISBN: 978-1-6642-2724-8 (e)

Library of Congress Control Number: 2021905093

Print information available on the last page.

WestBow Press rev. date: 05/21/2021

PREFACE

I have a friend with a sticker on his snowboard that reads, "Ignoring Jesus is choosing hell." I knew he was not religious, so this sticker was not what he felt to be a matter of fact, but one of criticism—a criticism that drives into the heart of the faith. I wanted to ask him about what he thought the sticker meant. I weighed the possible routes the conversation might take if I asked him. Perhaps our chat would be fruitful, or hostile, or a bit of both. I then remembered a section in the Bible where Jesus encourages His followers not to worry about what to say when they are questioned—with this in mind, I moved forward. The polite nature of our disagreement was like a reengagement in a battle that has been handed down from generation to generation. It was as serious as revolution, and counter revolution. But which revolution did the sticker signify, and which does it signify now?

This book is an elaboration on that conversation, with an outcome which I can only guess at. In no way is this book meant to provide the answer, but to show that there is an answer, not one which I am able to come up with on my own. More importantly, there is a question, and that means something different than what we are told almost daily—that the question has been answered. There are many symptoms of the question, and many people who think they have an answer to the question. But sometimes the answer someone thinks they have is just another restatement of the question in the form of an assertion, like a sticker that makes a stark proclamation, but is only actually symptomatic of a condition. The condition is the question at hand. In the age of unlimited answers, the question has never been more visible.

For a friend and family, from beginning to end.

COME AS A CHILD

Truly wonderful the mind of a child is.

—Yoda

Our age is riddled with skepticism toward the existence and identity of God. Objective truth is up for debate. People are becoming unsure about everything around them. The feet of civil and spiritual society are indeed on shaky ground, and the disparity between faith and doubt is popular in thought while divisive in nature. But in the battle between worldviews, one side *must* emerge victorious. If it is a battle for the ultimate discovery of what is true, then the victorious worldview must be on the side of truth, especially if it goes against the grain of popular opinion or seems contrary to the *natural* division of human nature.

In my search and struggle for faith, I have found many reasons to trust in God, much more than I am capable of explaining in the pages that follow. I am not an expert in the following subjects, nor am I completely naïve. My aim is to approach them by walking the fine line between naivety and pride, or of complacency and divisiveness. Perhaps the pages will emerge organically for the reader as well as for me and will refrain from robotic reiterations, heretical mysticism, or self-righteous legalism. It is by wonder that human beings have navigated the more troubling terrain of faith and doubt and ended up at a place they did not expect. As long as the weary traveler does not stand in the void of their inherited indifference where they were before, a journey will have taken place.

The following pages will examine both objections to and reasons for the Christian faith through the lenses of the Christian and the skeptic. I have been both of these at one point or another. Now I am not much of a scholar in theology, but still the closest thing to an infant in the faith. I reclaimed my childhood after wandering the vast continents of adulthood, with all the contradictions and confusion therein. At one point or another, I have been a professing Christian who was plagued by skepticism, a skeptic who was overwhelmed by a desire for something more, a sinner with a need for freedom, and a Christian still faced with many tough questions and counterintuitive desires. So, this book is intended to be for anyone, and I hope that in some way it will help everyone who happens to read it—from the Christian who is afraid to face any hard questions, as I sometimes am, to the skeptic who's skeptical about skepticism itself.

I remember, as a child, the first time approaching the idea of God in a *sensible* manner. Though I attended church every once in a while, the themes of life, school, and culture already seemed to suggest an undeniable absence of God. I still remember the theme of my words. It was a mostly sunny day, and I was riding my bike with a friend. When we stopped down the street from my house and the sun glared above us, I asked him, "What if there is no God?" I was becoming *educated* into the sensibility of modernity and into adulthood. My friend responded by acknowledging that, just like Santa Clause, there probably isn't a God.

The older I got, the less interested I became. Somehow along the way, however, I turned back the clock. My aim in the following pages is to invite others not simply to believe my account but to do a little seeking and wondering of their own—even if it goes against the current of culture. At times, an honest answer may infringe on the rights of the individual, like the right to the pursuit of various pleasures, or the right to remain right even if one is wrong. And many of these answers may seem countercultural, counterintuitive, contradictory, or controversial. They did for me and still challenge some of the habits of my old self. Sometimes I still feel like I am shedding a part of my humanity as I learn more about Christianity. As I move forward, I realize that the aspect of our *humanity* Christ truly invites us to shed is actually our inhumanity and the abandonment of innocence. How to get the child back is the question so many of us long to answer. That question, in part, is the aim of this project.

At some point in my life, I traded light for dark, and my nostalgia revealed the past as the illuminated path. Little did I know that my past was illuminated by simplicity. If we were only believing lies in our past and now have found our way to the truth, why do we so often look backwards as though we knew the truth better back then? Are we really so much more sensible now? Or have we only grown more foolish as life has become more complex for complexity's sake? The Book of Hebrews describes faith as a belief, hope, and certainty in the things we cannot see. Therefore, what the Christian believes in is as out of this world as the notion of time travelling to the simple past so many long for. For this reason, faith becomes childlike and foolish to the sensible world. To the sensible world, the believers may even appear to be out of their minds, while it is the sensible, educated person who is always ending up on the side of truth.

What in God's eyes is more sensible? I hope that this book will look into that question and challenge everyone to rethink, wherever they may be, whether where we stand—beneath the impressive pinnacle of modernity—is really more sensible than the foundation God has already laid down for us in His Word.

Children see things with a sense of either incredible wonder, terror, or unshakeable indifference. A thing simply matters very much to a child or it doesn't matter in the slightest. A child is rarely neutral; they either love something or outright reject it. A toddler will probably enjoy his new toy more than his basic addition flashcards. Obviously, it would be a stretch to say that a child only does what is right all of the time. I am only trying to suggest something more ancient than misbehavior. Observing children in their enviable openness can often shed light on an adult's loss of the spark. Perhaps a midlife crisis is simply realizing that we've lost the joy of playing in the park with our friends a long time ago, and that we are much more sensible now. We know that there is no river of lava beneath the monkey bars, and to run the wrong way up the slide would be to take an unnecessary risk of slipping and falling. We no longer chase one another through the schoolyard, yelling, "You're it!" The bell rang. Recess is over, and the class of the sensible has begun.

There is a longing among people to return to the parks of their childhood in order to rediscover that time when the things they imagined at that park were the most real things to them, more real even than the hunt for things like fortune and notoriety. At times, looking backward can lead one on a journey forward either to challenge the way things have come to be or to preserve something that already is there and is worth protecting. As we grow more *into our humanity*, we sometimes grow sillier, abandoning our youthful dreams of friendship and powers beyond the imperfect universe of the sensible. We trade the playground for the factory or the office, becoming business men and builders rather than the *imago dei* creators we once were. We fear that if we return to the park and go up or down the slide, we may end up in a muddy puddle with a scrape on our elbow, so we eliminate the risk entirely by setting the park off limits.

When I became too sensible, I had to reexamine why I left that park so long ago, and hopefully find out what true folly and wisdom really were. As I look back on my downward-sliding life and the muddy puddle that awaited me below the new and even more slippery slide, I realize that what I once abandoned as childhood folly was in a sense my truest wisdom and an expression of recognizing new life, at once more ancient and eternal. I lusted so much for the knowledge of the world that I ultimately became just another fool within the world, running here and there in a futile search for fulfillment. I tried so hard to evolve into a man that I was given the mind of a beast. Looking back, I was the most myself when I was the most impressionable and when I believed in the unbelievable. I was much more brilliant and hopeful when I was expecting a miracle to happen, for God to shake my room or make a candy bar appear. I was the most foolish when I no longer believed these miracles could happen. I sacrificed what was exceptional for the status quo.

There was a reason that Christ told his disciples that no one may enter the kingdom of heaven unless they came as a child. The little children are the ones we are constantly fighting to release from the prisons we have built for them. Ironically, they are also the ones we are constantly trying to lock back up as soon as they come out for fear that they will overthrow our sensible selves. All the money, greed, power, and lust is really just a cover-up for our desire to experience true joy again. We see this true joy in children and envy them for it. That's why we buy six motorcycles and still feel discouraged. We punish children because they are much better believers than we are—and much more frank. They act as men and women ought to act, for falsity is still far from them. When they have been wronged, they cry out to their fathers and pound their fists on the ground. When they enjoy themselves, they run laps around the house until they fall fast asleep. They are caught in an unintelligible epic poem, too powerful for all the words of the wise men of this age to tell. They see the world as it is and fight hard to keep the things they love. The sensible adult world does all it can to remove this annoying element of the child, to clone itself in the child. The closer the child's joke is to reality, the harder they are slapped on the hand for it. The more overjoyed or enraged they are, the more they are disciplined. They are trained away from their *misbehavior*, which can often be the most normal behavior. The child must finally learn to behave in a way that suits the world around them. Their dreams are suppressed until they are formed into more orderly beings. They no longer ruffle anyone's feathers or speak their minds frankly but are quiet and polite. They have learned not to cry out to their father in anguish when they are hungry or thirsty but to say, "Yes, please," and "No, thank you." The ancient relics that were once in their grasp are left behind as they grab the tools they need in order to become more like the version of themselves the world wants them to be. They realize the shame of their own nakedness and hide.

I am not advocating against discipline or encouraging blatant misbehavior in children. But the child and the adult strikingly illustrate the story of the garden, when things were as they ought to be and worked hard against nature to become as they ought not to be. Who were we really chasing after when we left the park?

RECOLLECTION AND OBSERVATION

So, till the judgement that you yourself arise,
you live in this and dwell in lover's eyes.

—William Shakespeare

Isaac Newton observed the invisible agent gravity when he saw an apple fall to the ground. Biologists are able to observe the cellular structure of organisms and organ tissues as the basic building blocks of life. Darwin observed the movements, nature, appearance, diversity, and behavior of life on earth in order to formulate his theory about what gave life to life. Copernicus revolutionized the astronomical canon when he took a closer look at the nature of the cosmos. The world observed the hidden power inside the atom when they watched the first atomic bombs detonate. All of these were revolutionary ideas, and to some extent, many of the methods of human reasoning and existence still operate based on aspects of them, or suffer from the consequences of them. We certainly all live in the wake of their reality.

In order to paint a picture of a green tree, one must first observe the color green and then mix the colors yellow and blue together to make green paint. Before revolutionary ideas were discovered, they remained invisible to the naked eye, just like the green nature of the colors blue and yellow. These ideas may have been hidden dreams lying in wait for a child to come and paint with them. Yet all of them share something in common: they began with belief and were accepted by faith. These two components were necessary to create the fact. They are now considered common knowledge. Could the existence of a *specific* God be likewise substantiated as fact by faith? Do those who believe in the God of the Bible believe in Him with good reason or based solely on wishful ignorance? God is invisible, so far as we know. Yet I consider that He may be more identifiable than the modern theories brought forth by science and philosophy. I say this because nothing within nature or reasoning can be demonstrated without an invocation of some of the attributes of God's character. He meant all of nature, which is His creation, to be reflections and shadows of who He really is.

Take for example the phenomenon of genuine disagreement as to what pertains to the truth, like whether or not smoking cigarettes is good or bad for a person's health. If the disagreement is genuine on both sides, both sides generally consider their argument to be *true*. They are arguing truthfully to the best of their knowledge. Yet, by nature, the truth can only side with one of them at any point in time, even if the force of the argument fluctuates between those who argue and may sound more compelling coming from the person who is wrong. The truth cannot be divided against itself by its nature.

If the reader doesn't smoke cigarettes because he or she recognizes the dangers of smoking, even if everyone around the reader smokes constantly and nags the reader about the social benefits of smoking, the truth about the physical repercussions of smoking cigarettes is nonetheless the dominant truth, regardless of whether or not it sides with the opinion of the majority.

The same concept can be applied to the matters of theism and atheism. The truth must side with one or the other, although the effectiveness of the evidence may vary in the way that it is presented, especially if self-righteousness is involved. But if the truth sides with atheistic naturalism, then why is *arguing for the truth* even important? We are cosmic blips bumping into one another with our ultimately pointless opinions, nothing more. We are meaningless in our origin, existence, and destination. Being either right or wrong would not matter in the slightest. I do not think that all atheists consider that true, but that is the catch-22. The *fact* that atheists agree with the existence of meaning and truth to some degree, when the ultimate destruction of these things is warranted by their worldview, demands explanation in an existence of chaos. The atheistic assertion of any standard of truth in a world bereft of objective truth rests in a *borrowing of the truth,* presumably from somewhere within the biblical paradigm.

Gravity, as far as we know, is a key player in keeping our universe and our world in stability. In this respect, it is a law of uniformity and would doubtless be the highest law of the natural order of things. We can argue that it is not and protest its dominion over us, but if we were to jump off a building, the truth will tell us that this law still exists regardless of our protesting it. Even in the midst of what some may deem random chaos, everyone exists under the same conditions in a relatively constant state. Theories about these conditions all focus on laws that exist regardless of our understanding of them. But law is by nature the opposite of chaos. An example of law— moral law—so far as naturalism explains, is derived solely from the individual and collective brain and is therefore purely subjective in its degree of governance and truthfulness. In its highest and most sophisticated form, secular law must have emerged from the least chaotic governing system in order to be effective for a society. Our universe likewise relies on laws that transcend human decision in order that it may not fall into chaos and impossibility. Humankind relies on some moral laws to avoid evil and injustice, to the best of its ability. Does the reliance on these universal laws and the demand for order on universal and societal levels imply a transcendent lawmaker?

The study of biology and genetics has led to many discoveries of the complex inner workings of cellular life, the smallest and most compact form of life. So far as one can see, these "basic" building blocks of life operate on incredible amounts of information with incomprehensible efficiency. This efficiency is governed by the *laws* of the information which allow the systems to operate. The complexity of information was somehow written into the cell and its biochemical components with infinitesimally small handwriting. Obviously, these are not laws which could have been written by human hands. They could not be written by humankind any more than the infinitely large letters of the laws of a consistent universe which allows life on earth. Yet from the microscope to the telescope, we see what the Bible told us thousands of years ago; the world hangs upon nothing (gravity), and the life of a creature is in in its blood (DNA). Even Darwin's theory needs the presence of law, albeit the law of natural, unintelligent, and unguided processes, to function as an explanation for everything. In observing the invisible or barely visible laws of nature which remain the thrust for the more visible man-made laws, as well as the undeniable presence of moral and natural law apart from human comprehension, from the sun and the stars to microbes and men, one comes to see that the existence of God—a transcendence outside of and behind what can be observed—is not only possible but probable. This is especially evident when the secular worldview presupposes day to day either something about God or something already written by God, all while denying His existence. This simultaneous denial of and borrowing from the Bible is cosmic plagiarism at its finest.

Admittedly, there is a fair intellectual distance to travel between scientific or philosophical thought that coheres with the existence of some God somewhere and the assumption that it can only be a specific God, which is *the* God of the Bible who fits the bill. Hopefully this project will succeed in at least partially bridging this divide; that is why it is called the best *guess*. It is impossible to think about such things without occasionally looking up at the muse of Judeo-Christian theology. After all, atheists often use the Bible to argue against it. So we're going to simply play by their rules.

Many minds are already made up about the logical impossibility, or at least the forthcoming improbability of God. But this skepticism arose by copious levels of evolving philosophical and naturalistic coaching. My goal for the time being is to present a few different items as symptomatic of the larger condition of creation. Inevitably, we should see that creation is likewise symptomatic of a creator, just as a fine cigar is symptomatic of a fine cigar shop. Atheism tells theism that theological indoctrination is really the biggest problem, and it is to be parried by tough questions and critical thinking. This standard ought to hold true for both sides. It may be less obvious to say that a book is evidence of the human hand than to say that the human hand is evidence of a higher handiwork, if we look hard enough at the hand, for the machinery in the human hand is much more complex than any book it could have written. To say that the handwriting of the hand was written by itself is a stretch—and this is excluding the presence of mind in the writing process, which adds another level of complexity. To say that the hand was created by itself is much more of a stretch of imagination and speculation. It still appears to be impossible to obtain a final product such as a book or a hand that writes it without both a production and a producer. In our nature, we must be one of three things: product, process, or producer. If we are a product, we couldn't have simultaneously been the producers of ourselves. If we are a process, then we can't imagine either our end product or our producer as we are only evolving blindly in the middle of the two. If we are the producer, then we are free to refashion creation after our own image and create life from nonlife—so far this hasn't been a promising enterprise.

The stubborn fact of life is that we are the product of a creative producer. Logic and imagination are not at odds with each other when they conclude that the intelligibility of creation indicates a source or creator. There is evidence of the unobserved within the observable, as there is evidence of an author behind the pages of this book.

What is seen often indicates what is unseen, almost always as a rule of cause and effect. This is the basic pattern of faith, but it is not limited to the Bible. The pattern of faith in what is unseen can be illustrated by many other things. For example, when you see countless stars in the sky, it is reasonable to assume that there are many more that cannot be seen, as implied by the word "countless." The fact that even the ones we can see cannot be counted indicates the likely existence of countless more.

In a search for a trustworthy universal model and a frantic race to be the explainers of everything, scientists and theorists have carried this idea even further: the landscape theory promotes the existence of countless universes *because* we can see our own, yet we cannot see it in full. The theist also sees our seen universe as the result of magnificent unseen intelligence, guided power, and creativity, rather than an infinite number of parallel realities and universes—a theory proposed by cosmologists to temporarily evade the theological implications of the harmony between heaven and earth.

Knowledge cannot operate without some degree of faith in what is unseen, even in the most mundane and unimpressive sense. An example being the knowledge of an existing geographical location such as Canada without the need to personally visit there—such knowledge comes by faith in a map of North America. Faith cannot operate without some degree of mystery, and mystery needs reality as its backdrop. Analyzing certain facts and statistics in order to report them needs to come by faith in the sources that provide those facts and statistics. Eating breakfast at a restaurant comes by faith in the cook to adhere to certain health codes and to cook the food all the way through. Faith is not a fallacy, even in the most common sense.

Facts that constitute reality and encourage mystery are mostly based on past and present conditions. Countless people live in and have visited Canada, even though I haven't personally visited Canada. Therefore, I can base my conclusion that Canada exists on the testimony of others. By morphing the observable and factual existence of Canada into the theoretical and mysterious existence of what one imagines Canada to be like, we create a certain level of mystery behind Canada—and a paradigm in which to place our faith in both the existence and conditions of such a place, which excludes neither the physical reality of it nor the metaphysical idea of it. This is the simplest process by which the standard of reasoning behind both known and unknown is founded. Reason relies largely on mystery, and mystery ought to grow with the right kind of knowledge, or else it would be unreasonable.

We know that universal laws and standards have continued, are continuing, and will continue. We don't need to omnisciently observe all things in their constant state to know this. There is simply no reason to think otherwise based on past and present evidence. My home's electricity was on yesterday, is on today, and therefore it should be on tomorrow. The sun rose yesterday and today; it should rise tomorrow. Universal laws like gravity act like eternal absolutes to finite human beings, even though they are likely only finite constructs themselves, built by one who is actually infinite. What we call infinite only appears infinite to us because we cannot truly grasp infinity, though we infer it all the time. Humanity's quest to further scientific understanding is telling of our hunger for absolute knowledge, absolute power, and our reach toward infinity. Yet this hunger has yet to be satisfied. There will always be more to learn and more to doubt. But we need the mystery to continue to exist.

When Charles Darwin formulated his theory about the origin of complex life on earth, he had far less of an ability to view the complexities of the smallest forms of life. Today, technology gives us the ability to see things that are both incredibly far away and incredibly small. Scientists are realizing more and more that the amount of information needed to build cells and allow them to operate is incomprehensible. We can no longer ignore the complexities of the smallest forms of life. There are enormous biochemical hurdles for the theory of natural selection acting on random mutations to overcome. How can we discredit agency and will in such complex systems? Our knowledge is incomplete from molecules to our own hearts, and from the earth to the cosmos. Humans simply do not hold in their hands the absolute standards for everything, and as soon as they think they do, it is likely that they are headed for a reality check. They never will discover the exact methods of the production, especially after forsaking their nature as products. The knowledge of good and evil was never intended. Our hunger to find answers in anything and everything besides God reveals our desire to be our own designer, despite the mounting evidence to the contrary. Once we become our own designer, we become the new arbiters of moral authority and the new definers of the absolute. Theologians likewise cannot have total mastery over scripture, and historically there has proven to be danger in the desire to reach it. To stretch out our hand toward the skies in order to rewrite our own absolutes is to question the ones that already exist and the one who set them in their place. This flaw is something as ancient, as *normal,* and as *unnatural* as the first rational argument against God's law. This sin was born from a quest for absolute knowledge and power, which could only result from doubt concerning the absolute knowledge and power that God already had. Humankind's unquenchable thirst to drink what was and is always will be poisonous, its ambition to reach the unreachable, and its denial of the beginning of the very absolutes it seeks to rewrite all reveal something fundamental about the relational nature between God and humankind. This nature fills the pages of our history and philosophy books. It permeates our languages and propels the force of culture. It still aptly fits into three letters.

When Darwin scraped the bottom of the barrel for the beginning, he ironically sought total uniformity of the natural order of science by invoking the agents of total chaos and random chance. His achievement brought the entire scientific worldview under one new and sovereign order, the absolute and unquestionable dominion of scientific materialism. So much of modern thought repeats this pattern and, in so doing, paves the way to life that prohibits God. In the wake of "absolute knowledge," humans will always hunger for absolute truth, even when they can't stand the smell of it.

A simple yet striking evidence for an eternal God can be found in the endless arguments that arise like clockwork throughout the generations, arguments both for Him and against Him, and the ongoing patterns these arguments consist of. The war rages on. Two ancient characters fulfilled this dichotomy; Satan came into the world to undermine the authority of God's Word, Jesus Christ came in order to demonstrate it. The intellectual chasm between their two worldviews, so to speak, can be as wide as the distance between heaven and hell. Satan and sinful man dug the trench in the book of Genesis, and Jesus built the bridge in the New Testament.

Christianity is observable only in the context of its reality, as we'll see later. The story tells us that there is a stunning relation between the way in which humankind thought about God in both the first and the last days. Scripture adequately explains that the rational disconnect between God and humans has existed all along.

The story of sin and redemption is repeated throughout all of human history. It is as universal as it is controversial. Sin and redemption is a story that can't help but be told over and over again. It is at the root of all we desire to know, all of our achievements, all of our problems. But it can't be holistically known apart from the worldview that it emerges from. The patterns of nature and humankind are evidence of biblical accuracy. The undeniable challenges and evils that face the world, as well as our search for truth and meaning within these challenges and evils, fit better within the biblical paradigm than the chaotic paradigm. One cannot escape the weight of things that are invisible yet undeniable, like the advancement and absurdity of nihilism. The mosaic of Christianity shows everything in a different light, the light of the truth of God. He calls us to face the hardest questions in life and does not dismiss them as unimportant. For these are questions that are universally and fundamentally human. The Bible accurately faces the issues of humanity, religion, philosophy, psychology, history, origin, destination, and so much more. It uniquely and aptly approaches each issue without minimization. It grants insight, correction, and hope in a way that no other human philosophy does. Scripture shows the truth of our existence, and our existence shows the truth of God, as well as our faulty thinking.

The Bible tells us that in Christ *all things* consist—from the genetic information and complexity found in one cell to the culmination of human history. When God is stripped of His meaning and taken out of the imagination of the soul, there is a loss of consistency in life's texture. It is then that the godless worldview must borrow certain foundational, invisible truths that can only be found in things obviously designed by God. Even Darwin searched for the beginning at the beginning, where the Word was all along. He knew what was told in the beginning of scripture was true—that there was an origin. For one to discover the meaning of evil in the world, they must first acknowledge the evil within themselves, which is the most naturally unnatural inclination of the human heart. There are always two choices, so we all have an equality of choice. In the garden of Eden, there were two entities, continued freedom from sin and knowledge of good and evil. The first absolute presented to humanity was absolute freedom. Humankind questioned whether that freedom was indeed absolute and destroyed it in order to find its purer and more potent form.

When observing a tree for a few moments, one cannot see that it grows, yet it is known by faith in our knowledge of trees that it does. This is a deduction about what is both invisible and undeniable based on everything we know about trees. Knowledge always relies on the invisible. The growth of living things is a universal truth no matter one's age, education or spirituality. All it takes is common sense. One can state with confidence that a tree has grown. After all, its very existence indicates its growth. To say that every action has a reaction is a profound statement of faith that relies on certain invisible laws. Between the two objects of cause and effect, there is often no quantifiable or even observable link. However, we can be sure that there was both a cause to finite creation and an effect of God's infinite power and creativity. There was also a prideful reaction on the part of those within the finite creation to His infinite sovereignty and authority. His subjects at least demonstrated their limitations in their rebellion and highlighted God's immutability and infinity. This is still the case.

A CLEAR VISION OF THE PAST

Then all the king's wise men came in,
but they could not read the writing
or tell the king what it meant.

—Daniel 5:8

THE STORY OF HUMANKIND APPEARS to have elements of literary composition. When we hear the stories of the rising and falling of empires, we can't help but think of the meaning that might be found in their ruins. A lesson can be learned from every age, good or evil. Each nation, like a person, experiences the lessons of life and may either reject those lessons or learn from them. Each is prone to the knowledge of good and evil. Civilizations are therefore formed and destroyed like sandcastles in the rising tide. Each empire reveals its wisdom and folly to the eyes of humanity, so that humanity may realize what happened. Otherwise, we are doomed to repeat our failures. The ruins of the ancient civilizations show the divine origin of cosmic discipline, fated by the power that raised them. Scripture relentlessly warns and promises that the power of God will humble us if we continue to rebel and not walk uprightly. Every child with a good father knows this story, and so does every criminal who had an impartial judge. The child knows the temptation of the forbidden cookie jar and ignores the dangerousness of the way it is precariously placed on top of the fridge. The thief knows the temptation of grabbing the old lady's purse and darting off the train but weighs the possibility of being arrested. Previous falls from the countertop are sometimes not enough to stop the child from disobeying his parents, and neither were years behind bars enough to stop the thief from stealing again and again after he got out of jail. In the same way, each nation knows the temptation of turning from God and many know the pain that comes by continuing on that path. The doom of the nations before them were not enough to scare newer nations into their wits.

Without God, we are free to be our own judges, and the judges of one another, with no accountability, responsibility, or objectivity. The force of prophecy works with its ally, history, to warn us of the causes of punishment by showing sin's ruinous effects, and the cost of humanity being its own ultimate judge, jury and executioner. Reading these prophecies now helps us to see why the dead nations were warned, and to know that we who are still living stand warned as well. Every crime deserves justice. But when the highest justice is the state's justice—the law of humans—the naturalist's argument is proven: humankind becomes the ultimate judge between right and wrong, writing laws as flexible as the individual's own bending morality or the ever-shifting collective morality of the public. Yet we see in the pages of our Bibles God's promise to enact justice on humankind for the continued deconstruction of His definitions. His words promise that our world's deconstruction of His words will result in the destruction of our worlds. Indeed, this already happened. When we obeyed the serpent's criticism of one of God's sentences, we were sentenced to obey the new law written in the constitution of our destruction. The visions of God against the nations He condemns are written and spoken even as these nations often flourished, thus the prophecies sounded at times like madness to the contemporaries of the prophets. With the help of God, prophets like Isaiah realize disasters that have yet to take place, yet we see horrors like them fill the photographs of our more recent past. Biblical prophecies were warnings of the consequences of rejecting

God. These consequences were taken seriously by nations who had seen God's power at work before. Today, we often do not heed the warnings of God, as we live in a culture that encourages us to disregard them. How do we respond to His invitations and heed His warnings, which are increasingly laughed off as outdated, especially in the new pseudo-prophetic age of information without wisdom?

The child that disobeyed his father by eating the cookies realizes after falling off the counter and plummeting to the cold, hard floor that his father predicted the future in his warning. The father did this by asserting at once his love, his law, and the promise of discipline upon transgression of that law—all the while being fully aware of his son's desire for cookies. The law of prison was remembered by the thief before he stole the old woman's purse. His future was also foretold by a law that contradicted his desire to continue stealing. The bars slamming shut in front of him were therefore as natural, unstoppable, and destructive to his future as the laws of the universe; the only difference is that he was allowed to make the decision whether or not to transgress this law. The authority of judge and jury were no longer questioned. In God's eyes, the fall of Rome and other nations in similar patterns were likely as predictable as tonight's sunset.

Prophecy in the New Testament is the most sought-after gift. It consists of powerful poetry, future visions, terrifying premonitions, and eternal truth. Biblical prophecy is filled with beautiful and terrifying literature about humankind's struggle and salvation. Often, the messages deeply frustrate and confuse those facing accusation. Prophecy has the power to plunge us all deeper into that confusion, or to bring us out of the depths of transgression and into the knowledge of our creator. Biblical prophecy therefore can be either an enigma of manifold complexity or a statement of universal simplicity—it can be the tree with all its branches and leaves or the single seed from which the tree grew. For some, like the thief, the law must be explained in full again and again, with little effect. For the child, the simple fall may have finally been enough to make him fear his father's law. The unfolding of prophecy must be an amazing and chilling thing to behold, for we see that God has already written the pages of our history books.

It is impossible for people to tell the story of prophecy in full. Even for Jesus, to tell the story was also to live it, and ultimately die to fulfill it. One could fill books with the meaning of just one biblical prophecy, let alone make them all fully known. When Joseph was shown the future in his dreams and was able to interpret the dreams of Pharaoh, he was put in a position of great power—with the interpretation given to him by God, Joseph was able to save nations and to form the exposition of the Exodus of Israel.

The believers have always looked upon these ancient prophecies through the lens of their truth in regard to actual history, human nature, and the weight of God's promises and warnings. Jeremiah begs God to curse the day he was born because of the recurring message of doom and gloom that he is tasked to deliver to Israel—a message which includes a relation of the historical fall of Jerusalem, Israel's stubbornness and hardness of hearing, and God's authority to bring about the punishment of Israel to repay them for generations of disobedience. Standing in the wake of these messages, dreams and visions as well as their meaning as they unfold throughout history, one can easily recognize how accurate God's predictions really are—a powerful device for authenticating the true nature of scripture.

When looking upon the ruins of ancient Rome and reading the accounts of the ages of various conquerors who sought to deify themselves and subsequently fell, we see the pattern of pride coming before the fall on an individual and national scale. The temptation of power and the desire to be gods, scripture warns, is a surefire way to stumble toward destruction. There is nothing written in the accounts concerning such promises and warnings apart from the recognizable handwriting of God Himself, no matter how much people want to forge that handwriting in forming their own destinies—while denying the presence of any authority who is seated higher than human history.

When the beast rises out of the ocean in Revelation, we see a creature of the future formed by pieces of the past, wondering where we stand in relation to it. More importantly, we catch a glimpse of the way in which God views the various superpowers that humanity is so prone to put its trust in—as terrifying beasts who seek only destruction. Are we those who will bow down to these cultural powers?

Prophecy convinces us of God's irrefutable control, and the consequences of following the chaos of our own hearts. His relationship with us as God and Father is highlighted in His communication with humankind via prophecy from age to age. The ordering and fulfilling of prophecy ought to at the very least instill a fear of God into us, a gratitude for His salvation, and a desire to turn to Him and follow. Unfortunately, sometimes the truth only alienates more if one is addicted to a lie.

Prophecy unmistakably blends and unites all the evidence for God. It stands still to prove the authority and the accuracy of His words, showing that the working out of His plan is undeniable. King David sang of God's signature in the skies when he cried out that the heavens declare God's handiwork. Isaiah and Ezekiel spoke of Christ when they spoke of punishment and triumph for Israel, as well as God's plan to bring all nations to Himself. They spoke also of the destruction of many kingdoms and the exile of Israel. They spoke of the destruction and exile of the human mind and heart when standing in opposition to God. King David reveals the true and irreducible sanctity of human life, even in the womb, when he realizes that God knew him and knit him together inside his mother. Today, society scoffs at the idea of the sanctity of human life in the womb.

At times, the stories that make up the Bible themselves act like prophecy. Adam's sin foreshadowed the sin of all, and those who recognize sin see its common elements first arise in Adam's story. Humankind still stands in the shadow of a single act of disobedience. There is no better explanation, example, and definition of humankind's flawed heart than the first act of people toward God. Story after story, from Adam to Paul, tell of the same human condition, without explaining the condition away as a psychological or sociological phenomena. Genesis chapter 3 is the first account, case study, and diagnosis of the human hostility toward God and ability to degenerate which has always plagued us. The redemption for such a spiritual plague is shown in people like the apostles and many other people in history through the salvation which came from their master, Jesus Christ.

Christ assures us, both prophetically and demonstratively, that there is certainly much more than a grave after death, and there is certainly more than a slap on the hand after sin. God likewise always told the truth about the fall of people and the nations they inhabited, showing the inescapability of such a destructive pattern without His direct intervention. Some enter the grave with hope fulfilled, and others will find the truth of death fulfilled when they face the God they've chosen to reject. Given prophecy's accuracy, there is either infinitely more to hope for or far more to dread—even in our advanced 21st century society. Prophecy still grounds the authority of scripture through the unique style of God's promises. It shows the reliability of scripture as it unfolds throughout God's fabric of time. The Bible simply would not be a trustworthy document if it had no prophetic accuracy.

Prophecy alone should innately cause us to value the Word of God for what it is, the truth from beginning to end, and the truth over the beginning and the end. The life, death, and resurrection of Christ were told by many prophets long before His life on earth began. It is only through the lens of prophecy that His identity can be scrutinized and authenticated, and it is by His words that our future is told. Jesus foretold the sufferings that the early Christians would face because they chose to follow Him and warned of a deeper spiritual suffering that would take place if they chose not to. He foretold the challenges Christians may still face today in an increasingly secular time. Prophecy can serve to deter one from godlessness and evil if it is taken seriously. As we see in the writings of scripture, the nations that did not take God's word seriously are promised soon to crumble altogether. The actions of nations and peoples are always remembered and they are always repaid. Imagine if Newton's apple had forgotten to fall; imagine if Adam's stayed where it was.

The Psalms of King David and the Proverbs of Solomon prophetically show the condition of the human heart and mind. Their wisdom tells what it means both to truly be human and to truly know God—to immensely fail and immensely succeed. They prove the secular philosophies concerning the human condition to be little more than obsolete myths, and where they are more, they are more because they cohere with the ancient descriptions of scripture. Such descriptions trip up the secular explanations and theories because the human condition cannot be explained apart from its condition in relation to God. The Psalms offer deep laments as well as statements of unexplainable joy without ever downplaying or discrediting such things as psychological phenomenon. The Proverbs likewise show that there is no undercutting of the soul's complexities, as God intended in design; "Each heart knows its own bitterness, and no one else can share its joy" (Proverbs 14:10). Prophecy shows that to ponder the mysteries of the heart and the scope of creation is hardwired into the human heart and that each person's pain and joy are experiences indiscernible and misdiagnosed by even the most elaborate explanations of the world. We are simply too complex to be adequately analyzed, then given a pamphlet and some pills to help overcome our condition. That is the way God made us.

God drew up the blueprints for the hearts of kings and kingdoms. He knew why they'd fail or thrive. He tells Jerusalem that she will be conquered from outside her walls in times to come because she was already conquered long ago from within. The way of God is not just a worldview to be judged and weighed by the shifting and relativistic heart of humanity. It is not another equal choice on the buffet line of manufactured spiritualties, but the only way to live. Jesus said that apart from Him, we can do nothing. If we go in it alone or trusting other gods, we are like dead branches, to be picked up and thrown into the fire. Of course, it is natural that heroes may face misfortune and cowards may become rich, contradicting our earthly sense of justice, but the evil of people and the nations they create will be shown for what it is, in this life or the next. There is no mystery that God leaves unexplained.

Today, we still stand warned of the dangers of human ignorance and wickedness. The cross itself is a prophecy fulfilled that spans from beginning to end, which blends warning and promise. Christ showed that He covered all and is capable of covering all still with His sacrificial and redeeming love. On the cross was the culmination of history and its interpretive key in God's Son. From cover to cover, true understanding and fulfillment in both the book of God's words and the book of God's works resides within the Author of those books.

CUSTOMER SERVICE REPRESENTATIVES

What if some did not have faith? Will their
lack of faith nullify God's faithfulness?

—Romans 3:3

MAHATMA GANDHI SAID, "I LIKE your Christ, I don't like your Christian." Real transformation as a result of the Gospel is one of the great evidences for the reality of Christ. But the hypocritical Christian can point people in the opposite direction of the faith more efficiently than anything else. How would it look if I was trying to convince you of the genuineness of Christianity, when I'm not being genuine at all in the way that I live? However, in brief defense of the Christian, the notion of Christian hypocrisy is often culturally or historically blown out of proportion by those who have taken aim at the faith, or used as an imprecise excuse by the one who'd rather not follow, hanging on some notion of Christian misbehavior to bludgeon the possibility of what Christianity would mean for them if true. True hypocrisy, to the extent of it being practiced by true followers, as a deterrent from the faith may be rarer than the world makes it out to be, depending on who makes the accusation and for what reason. The history of the faith is often scrutinized through a vague and partial lens, especially when that scrutiny is primarily meant to reinforce certain presuppositions. This is not to say that many times the complaints against the Christian aren't legitimate on a personal and cultural level; "a little yeast works through the whole batch of dough" (Galatians 5:9). I do not wish to dispute genuine grievances like the inquisitions or the crusades or a negative encounter of a personal nature—all of these act as a stumbling block for many—but to talk about the importance of the role of the Christian individual and community in either proving or disproving their faith. Though many may feel offended by Christians or the church, many have also seen the fruit of the Spirit show through the lives of the redeemed. When I engage with someone who has a different worldview, I sometimes forget the power, either positive or negative, that their encounter with a believer can have. As I grow more, I become more aware of my mistakes, my folly and the weight of responsibility that my representation of the faith carries. The interaction that someone has with a Christian will either draw them toward Christ or repel them from the faith.

When I came to faith four years ago, it wasn't by systematically figuring out every issue of doubt floating around in the stratosphere, but it was largely thanks to the influence of "customer representatives" that I knew. People who truly follow Jesus can't help but represent Him in one way or another. Of course, we are often far from a mirror image of His love, humility, and authority. When you spend time with someone that you love and respect, you begin to emulate them. When you spend time with someone you don't respect, you tend to gravitate away from them. When considering if Christians really walk the walk, one ought to look at the book of Acts and the Epistles to see what walking the walk originally looked like. One ought to also see their Christian neighbors as representatives, while having a bit of common sense in remembering that we are humans, prone to make mistakes, not automatons. We occasionally let people down even though that is not what we are told to do, nor is it what we want to do. Also, it would do one well to remember that the Bible and the Christian are not interchangeable. When someone acts out of line, it doesn't disprove the overwhelmingly compelling case for Christianity; it only casts doubt on their genuineness. With this in mind, one may escape the endless void of personal criticism and honestly evaluate the claims of the faith without worrying too much about an individual's mistakes or misrepresentation.

These issues help us to recognize the difference between true and false Christianity and to judge the religion impartially. If we see people acting inconsistently with Christ's values and claiming the religion, it is harder to take them seriously, along with their worldview. When I desire help or guidance in my Christian walk, I usually turn to someone that I know strives to live consistently with the teachings of God's Word, and someone I trust. I don't pretend to absolve myself here. At certain points in my faith journey, I'm sure that I have been both the hypocrite and the follower. I have spoken to people about Jesus from both perspectives, and looking back, I recognize when I was being humble and helpful or arrogant and harmful. If I shared my faith from a clear conscience, my words were clear. But if I was living inconsistently, the message became muddied and unclear—from a place of knowledge, not love. It was always when I strived to love and follow Jesus more closely that my thoughts and messages became clearer.

Even the clear waters of the authentic church are human and imperfect. But this church indicates God's existence and character in its eternal desire to follow Him with increasing purpose and efficiency. Christians who truly follow Jesus really want to live a Christ like life through transformation. They find that this is extremely hard to do. Actually, it is impossible without the help of God. Scripture tells us that in this earthly body, the Christian, like the Israelite, will always struggle and fall short of the expectations of God. But every Christian has been given new life in Christ. When we are prone to fail and fall, Christ is sure to give us the grace to stand. A Christian may go one of two ways, up or down. If they are walking up the trail, they may tire and turn around. If they are going down the trail, they may desire to turn around and try again to make it to the top. One may look to Christ with increasing steadfastness and commitment, or satisfy sin and sink deeper and deeper into a life that illustrates that one is not serious about God—this shows through to the world more than they know. No matter where everyone falls on this spectrum, we all share one basic similarity: we are not Christ. But the scriptures tell us that this is so, that although we see Jesus and desire to be more like Him, we will be prone to struggle. As long as we are in this life, we will fall short. The mark of the Christian, therefore, is an ability to continue through this and to keep their eyes fixed on the hope of Christ, and His power and grace, not theirs, will thereby aid them in their goal.

Some may ask why we are so focused on the object of the violent and brutal death of the Son of God, why our religion is so dependent on the object of Christ's suffering. Why does the image of the cross bear so much weight for us? The answer is challenging yet simple. Christ took upon Himself the full weight of our sin on the cross, thus the whole of our being has that moment to thank. The more we see and understand this, the more we are naturally grateful for Christ. The more we ignore and forget it, the more we lose sight of the goal and slip backward into our old self. When we lose sight of our need for forgiveness and forget exactly how much it cost Him, we are in danger of no longer desiring to live as God's people. We begin to desire sin and the things of the world more and more.

When judging the genuineness of the Christian, one would do well to remember that each Christian is different; they are not always going to act the same. Christians are often rash and unpredictable, just like all humans are, especially when they are a product of a rash and unpredictable culture. They are not reproductions of one another. They are all at different stages in their spiritual journey—different levels of maturity, with different hopes, wishes, desires, gifts, and flaws. Like the development of a child to an adult, the true Christian's faith and ability to follow Jesus reflect their level of maturity, as well as the depth of their relationship with and reliance on God. Young Christians are often the most on fire and the most ready to believe.

They are also likely to struggle with temptation and sin, because they may underestimate its danger and reality. But as they grow in their faith, they come to new levels of understanding Christ's will for them. Either that or they slip backward into the old self.

Older Christians are sometimes more well-seasoned in their understanding. If they have followed faithfully, they are further along in godliness and the process of sanctification than they were when they began. Sometimes their wisdom and good sense appears to the young to be old-fashioned thinking. The young must remember that the old have faced many more battles. They know what is perilous to their spiritual journey and fellowship with God, and what is crucial. As they've developed, they've experienced success and failure, and they are more steadfast simply because they have known God for a longer time, which scripture commends. However, sometimes later on in our spiritual life, our relationship can feel less than it was when we were young, which scripture warns against. One may find oneself battling boredom or staleness in their religious efforts. Other times, God may test our faith by giving us a feeling of His absence, making us feel as though we are in a spiritual desert. This seemed to happen sometimes to King David, and in the case of Job, God at one point removed His physical and circumstantial protection of Job altogether *because* He knew Job had such great faith and wouldn't forsake the Lord, even when his life circumstances were devastated. However, in the book of Revelation, Christ rebukes believers who have grown stale in their faith and have "forgotten their first love." He also rebukes others who have become "lukewarm" in their faith and warns them that they are about to be spit out of His mouth if they do not repent. When we no longer feel passionate or invigorated by God, it is a serious issue. At times, it may be the Lord testing our faith, and at other times, it may be our lack of faith testing the Lord. In short, it is wrong for either the young or the old to look down on one another because of the differences in their behavior. Both fight the same fight, one with youth and vigor, the other with wisdom and humility.

People show love in different ways at different ages. A young child crowds his father and mother with unrestrained affection. An adolescent who loves their parents may have more trouble displaying that love emotionally; they may seem closed off, sullen or wise in their own eyes. The young adult, once moved out into the world on their own, standing on their own two feet, ought to love their parents and express gratitude for all that their parents have given them. Often, he or she comes to a realization of how much the parents loved them and sacrificed for them, especially when they were a teenager, swollen with passion and pride. Either this happens or they sink further into resentment. The archetypal father and mother, however, always love their child, even when the child is hard to love—ungrateful, dishonoring, or arrogant. They love the child through all these stages and quirks, in part by recognizing that they were once on a similar turbulent path of physical, emotional, and spiritual development. They picked the child up when he fell down, because they knew children lack the balance that adults have. They hugged the teen when she crashed the car, knowing that although she lacked judgement and responsibility in that moment, she needed the love and support of her parents. They encouraged her brother out of the house when he came of age, because although it makes them sad to see him go, they recognized leaving home would be the best thing for him. Such examples, again, are only generic, but they are meant to show the various ways in which the older show patience and love for the younger, often in ways the younger do not expect or disapprove of. They show discipline and affection when they are necessary. The models of good parenting during various stages of child development reflect why Christians are the way that they are spiritually, whether young or old, and why they are not always perfect people whether they are young or old.

A few warnings are quite simple and obvious, but I think they must be stated nonetheless: sometimes people who say that they are Christian may not actually be Christian, and some of the most passionate and devoted Christians may not walk around promoting and displaying their own Christianity. A few marks of the Christian will be their love and humility. When you speak with a Christian, is he or she genuinely interested in you? Do they seem to love you? Do they constantly boast about their achievements, or do they stay relatively and strangely silent about the things most people boast about? Is it evident that they love God? If they do show at least a few of these things, it is not because they are perfected in all love, humility, and godliness. Yet they are serious about cultivating the values promoted by the one they desire to emulate. Personally, I struggle to love my neighbor, to be humble, and to truly listen. I find these to be some of the more difficult challenges I face day to day. The entire story of sin, the fall, and the history of humankind can be seen in the battle between pride and humility. It is because of pride that until each person turns to God through Christ, he or she is essentially his or her own god. This is why it is necessary to write twenty centuries worth of theology and apologetics to answer all the multifaceted questions of the unbeliever as they arise generationally, even when there is a perfectly good Bible on their bookshelves that answers these questions more precisely—the Bible on the bookshelves often doesn't carry the answer desired by our pride or our flesh. It is not the endless list of doubts and objections that cloud the better judgment or the ability of a person to believe and trust in Christ, but it is his or her own pride manifesting as sin. It boils down to a desire to be equal with God (or to be above Him). Unfortunately, the specter of human fallibility doesn't entirely disappear upon conversion. Once again, all these answers of the fallible human heart and its redemption can be found in the accounts of the garden and the cross. The serpent's inquisition, "Did God really say?" still shows the most modern and advanced form of unbelief. Until we recognize the true source of our endless doubt and objections, we will not be able to believe a thing. This source is not to be blamed as outside ourselves.

The focus of Christians on the cross is a complete reversal of human desire. The cross will be discussed later in this collection, but

I'd like to touch briefly on the reaction of the Christian to Christ's death. The apostle Paul says that the cross appears as foolishness to the world, but it was actually the love, wisdom, mercy, and power of God all demonstrated in what appeared to be only weakness and foolishness to contemporary people. "What kind of power and cunning results in death?" they ask. "How does a gruesome and humiliating death prove the power and divinity of Christ?" The way in which a person views the answer to these questions indicates the kind of believer they are. The reaction to the cross of Christ is what it means to be Christian, or not to be. For on it was the fulfilment of God's love for the world. There is no other religion that offers this kind of redemption, and no other God who loves us so much. For the period at the end of our death sentence was found at Calvary. It is there that our old life sentence ended, and after that sentence our new story began through the redemption of Christ. This period is the foundation of our religion and fundamental to our worldview. A *truly* divine man, who followed God His Father all the days of His life, living the law to the letter, died for His enemies and liberated the world.

I also wanted to give a warning to Christians and non-Christians everywhere against what was once alive in Israel and is no further from the human heart now than it was then. This is what the Lord tells Jeremiah that the contemporary prophets were doing at that time (though this is not restricted to Jeremiah)—that is, prophesying subjective, ideological lies (Jeremiah 23). Today, I believe, though I am no expert, that there are many who claim a knowledge of and closeness to the Christian God that is largely conflated to suit their own passions and to promote themselves. They claim that He is always there for them, will do anything for them, and secretly talks to them and performs wonders through them. "God will make us rich, famous, and healthy." You know the like. These pseudo-Christians and false prophets have never been in short supply since the earliest church. After all, there has always been a large demand of information that soothes our own selfish ends while appearing to have come from God, giving us what our itching ears want to hear. This seems almost too simple to state, but for some, it is like nails on a chalkboard to hear: God is not answerable to you. He does not have to do everything you want Him to do. He does not have to explain Himself to you or me, or to anyone, and He certainly does not owe you anything. "'Am I only a God nearby,' declares the Lord, 'and not a God far away'" (Jeremiah 23:23). The sooner I realize that God is not a talisman, and does not need to bend to my will, the more my true relationship with the Father is strengthened, not only through proximity and comfort but by learning to respect and fear His reality, true identity, and holiness.

MULTIPLE CHOICE; LONG ANSWER; TRUE OR FALSE

> He took him outside and said, "Look up
> at the heavens and count the stars—if
> indeed you can count them." Then he said
> to him, "So shall your offspring be."
>
> —Genesis 15:5

THE NATION OF ISRAEL WAS not always the fittest, so how did it survive in Darwinian terms? It was not always the most powerful, the wisest in the eyes of the world, or the most successful nation. The Israelites were often the most hated people, facing the most persecution of any other nation or body of peoples. In the last century alone, the Nazi regime tried their hardest to exterminate them; communism—built on the philosophy of a man who also hated Jews, Karl Marx—swept over the majority of the world. It still threatens the world today; now, radical Islam continues a terrorist crusade against Israel, and the American academe continues to reproduce a rabid distain for Israel, as well as mock the traditional morality implicit in the Judeo-Christian worldview. This is nothing new, nor did it begin with Hitler, Marx, or Rome.

Ancient Israel was often being hunted and attacked by neighboring states, as well as always being in danger of imploding due to irreverence. At times, its people were nomadic, threatened by starvation and annihilation. Whether they were sojourners or settled in their nationhood, they were constantly persecuted, for many different reasons but mostly because of their undeniable power—that is the power of their God. No nation or people has faced such a longevity of trials internally or externally. Their persecution rests in the very idea of who they are—a people treasured by God. For this reason, they were and are mocked, envied, and hunted. They have been cursed at, spit on, beaten, murdered, slaughtered, exiled, laughed at, and accused more than most races or nations—even up until today. It is good to look to the Bible for insight to their history, and only here can one find a convincing history to the flawed glory that is Israel and Judah. The Bible was written by Hebrews. Their evolution as a nation was not a series of clever metaphors. It was a well-preserved relation of their origins, religion, traditions, history, and—most importantly—their God.

I believe that any person who considers themselves a Christian ought to consider the history of Israel with fear and respect, and the implications its history has for modern Christianity, whether in their contrasts or similarities. The account of Israel is like the story of every man and woman of faith—loved by God, in need of redemption, and held in high expectation. Israel's is the story of the tragic hero. Both the church and the Hebrews were held by God in contrast to the surrounding cultures and nations. Their way of life, their culture, and their traditions were formed exclusively and bound to the law and expectations of God, as well as the traditions of their fathers. When they embraced certain practices, namely worshipping foreign and fake gods, their relationship with God suffered, and so did their power, reputation, and authority in the eyes of others. This still applies to the person of faith on a smaller scale. The faith of the individual can have an unparalleled glory or failure similar to that of Israel. Either way, an individual's faith or hypocrisy sends a clear message to others, as discussed in the previous chapter. The depth of human history with God, whether in Israel or the church, can be measured by these eternal and reemerging glories and failures. The glory of the victory of Israel over her wicked neighbors corresponds to the glory of the victory of the truth over sin's deceitfulness through Christ's life, death and resurrection. These themes of triumph echo in theology and human nature. They are hardwired into us on the individual and national scale. So is the ability to fail, continuing to show imperfection under law. Faith and human fallibility show through prominent biblical figures like Abraham and David. These characteristics have continued through the spiritual life span of the nation they founded. At times, its faith was a flickering flame in danger of perishing in the winds of the times, while its rebellion filled the streets of the cities with blood, as in Manasseh's reign. At other times, Israel did not rebel, and its faith remained full in the face of many challenges. Israel's story is so compelling because it still holds the answers to the biggest questions of humankind. The story has yet to be concluded.

Any good story needs a few structural components. There has to be a protagonist, an antagonist, a struggle between them, and the ultimate triumph of good over evil. These elements interact with one another in every story. The most lasting stories echo the simplicity of this basic story frame. Sometimes our expectations and interpretations of the story can be reversed so we root for an antihero or are complicit in the justification of wickedness, which is often the case in culture nowadays. The history of Israel cannot stand with God extracted, or its struggle with God, just as a good story cannot exist without struggle. The Israelites would never have survived without God, for it was God who gave them the promises. They lost their very identity every time they turned from Him, and they gained knowledge and power every time they turned to Him. God was not just a pipedream or a paradigm, a mythological addition to boost the philosophical morale of an otherwise unimpressive people, a principle which seems to be implied in culture nowadays. This myth would be a fairy-tale hope, and would not have resulted in the nation's supernatural and unique survival. The God of Israel was not a legend formed to create and sustain a national culture and heritage so that they could compete with the surrounding nations' worldviews. Instead of seeing the historic heroes of the Old Testament create and deal with a mythical deity, we see a very real deity create and deal with them. God is the writer of the story of Israel, not the other way around. The more we understand this, the more we also see our own history as Gentiles outside the nation of Israel as only made possible by His hand.

The presence or absence of God is linked to every episode of Israel and the fluctuation of their spiritual well-being throughout time. He's their lifeline. Every episode is written to demonstrate the Hebrews' total reliance on God for survival and advancement, and to demonstrate what happens when they forsook that reliance. The book of Ezekiel shows us that the story of Israel is also the story of a young girl who was once an infant, naked and dying. She was adopted by a kind man who took her in as his own. She was well clothed and richly adorned by her adopting Father, only to turn away from him as she grew, prostituting herself again and again to other nations. Eventually, God allows her to fall into the hands of all the men she prostituted herself to, resulting in her tragic desecration and destruction.

Every story, great or small, shows God's character and providence, from the promise of Abraham to Goliath's broken skull, from the birth of Jacob to the passion of the Christ. These are not legendary accounts of titans and god-men who fought and won great battles before the foundation of humankind. They are accounts that interact with and sustain the pages of human history, great battles of God and humans. They tantalize the human desire to bridge fantasy, history, prophecy, and symbolism. This is why the Old Testament is not simply an exhaustive chronology but rather a choreography of history, prophecy, law, and poetry among other things which are impossible apart from divine inspiration. The most convincing piece of Hebrew history is the juxtaposition of all its pieces, all its language, mystery and form—and most of all, the humanity and divinity which are finally brought to a long awaited harmony through the life of the Messiah. This history still stands undefeated. As it stands, it is up to the reader to discover whether or not it's true.

Ancient Hebrew history shows an ongoing struggle with God and other nations. But like every person, Israel's greatest battle was within her own members. A nation can be torn down from within or without. Sometimes it is a bit of both. The rise and fall of Israel and her struggle to follow the God who saved her are deeply interwoven. God's prophecies spoke of downfall because of rebellion. The things that God spoke ultimately came to pass.

The prophecies of Israel both built the nation and broke it. During King David and Solomon's reigns, the nation was at its height of power, riches, wisdom, and favor with God. David's very real entrance as a humble shepherd who did the impossible and slew the mighty giant became a metaphor for the power of true faith on an individual and national scale. This attitude carried throughout his reign and long afterward. Israel was only able to flourish as a result of her faith. David battled and defeated many great foes, from predators that threatened his flock to warriors that defied Israel. He often fled from members of his own household, hiding and praying in the dark of the desert. But the greatest giant he ever faced was not a foreign or domestic enemy, but the giant of his own sin. He was a king notorious both for his unprecedented allegiance to his God and an unforgettable mistake. His sin can be weighed on a scale against all those enemies he faced, slew, and fled from, and still appear heavier than them all, even Goliath in his armor. One night of adultery cost him more than anything else, more than hunger, more than being hunted, more than facing a fearsome enemy without armor. Thankfully, David recognized his fallibility and repented, turning back to God. The traces of his mistake would haunt Israel for the rest of its days, as adultery against God became a theme among the kings and generations that followed. Israel would struggle to have no other gods before the Lord their God. Eventually, their power, riches, traditions, cultural wisdom, and long list of idols became more visible and tangible to them than the words of the living God who once delivered them from their bondage. This led to their prophesied and historical downfall.

God gave the Ten Commandments to His people, Israel. These commandments are still the foundational moral precepts in every human heart. They are innate within us, and we are innately prone to break them. Every person knows it is wrong to steal, kill, and destroy. From the beginning of our lives, God brought us naked out of our mother's wombs, much like the nation Israel in her vulnerable youth. Everyone observes God's work in the visible universe, so we are without excuse if we have other gods before Him. Yet, like the certainty of gravity, each person inevitably carves out their own image and bows to it in the place of God. Humankind's inexcusable patterns of behavior which result from their attitude toward God, which are outlined in His commandments, illustrate His reality. It is quite simple, apart from God we cannot love Him, no matter how much we claim to. The first four commandments therefore are all warnings and laws from God that address our fallen nature and our inability to follow God. Every human being is searching for the true fulfillment of knowing and loving God, yet we suppress this truth and trade it for a lie. Every person falls short of these expectations. The Hebrews were not exempt from this spiritual failure. Skeptics may ridicule the first four commandments because they are all focused on humankind's relationship with God and don't seem as practical in the real world as "thou shalt not kill" and "thou shalt not steal." They may not appear sensible in the here and now, apparently lacking social value or usefulness in lowering crime rates. However, in these commandments, God is telling us that He is the source of all of our being including our morality, and all human evil is only a reflection of our rebellion against the source. The way we act toward one another as we try to follow the second set of commandments will always be linked to the way in which we follow the first. If we take our eyes off of Him, we will fall away from His moral standards.

Our personal lives, our relationships, and our societies will suffer as a result.

Much of humanity operates with a notion of the second set of commandments. They have become a part of our evolutionary moral code, so to speak. It's fair to ask what would happen if a culture was to utterly disregard and disintegrate these principles because we no longer accepted the Bible as truth. The reduction of humanity to the "true freedom" of self-destruction, life without any of these guiding laws, would plunge us into chaos. God knew the perfect law to give to *His* people so that they would prove to the nations around them who God really was and the quality of His character. When we question God, His existence and His character, we also undermine our own sense of objective morality. When the first law falls in our hearts, the others tend to follow like dominoes.

The wisdom and poetry of the Hebrews is not like much modern poetry, which is mostly focused on exercising the intellect and imagination. Its goal is to understand the deepest issues and problems of the human heart—the height of human joy and the depth of human suffering. The wisdom in books like Job, Psalms, Proverbs, Ecclesiastes and Lamentations can be tragic and glorious expressions of the writers' relationships with God, and at times their alienation from Him. There can be deep trial or prosperity. These writings probe the depth of the human spirit and train us to keep our eyes focused on God, even when we are struggling to.

The history books of Israel aren't just history but contain literature that helps us to believe in God, not only with our intellect but with all of our faculties, while enriching our understanding of the time periods from which they came. They show us the importance of keeping God at the center of our culture and mind-set. These histories also illustrate what happens when we try to pull God out of our culture and personal lives. If we try to do this, sadly, God will ultimately let us have our way. Leaving us to our own devices and the rejection of His ways, He will let us drift away from all his attributes and into confusion, chaos, and evil.

A UNIVERSAL THIRST

Then we shall all, philosophers, scientists,
and just ordinary people, be able to take
part in the discussion of the question of
why it is that we and the universe exist. If
we find the answer to that, it would be the
ultimate triumph of human reason—for
then we would know the mind of God.

—Stephen Hawking

THE NIGHT SKIES ARE FOR doubt or certainty. They help us to know our own smallness yet ponder the deepest questions of life. They help us simultaneously to realize our own capacities, dream the possible, and be humbled by the understanding of our obvious limitations. The skeptic may point to the skies as proof of the smallness of humankind and see only, like Richard Dawkins, "blind pitiless indifference." The skies cannot help but show us our dependence, our vulnerability. Our earth is tinier than a grain of sand in the universe, as are we on the earth. If God really created everything, what makes humankind so important to Him in the vast skies? King David asked God, "What is man that you are mindful of him?" Though his question was likely from a viewpoint of faith and wonder, not of skepticism. King David probably spent many nights under the desert skies, on the run, and facing fearful trials. Today, modern thought concerning the skies is connected with Neo-Darwinism and illustrative of our own meaninglessness as a species, totally reliant as pure products of chance acting on matter. The theist sees the skies as a sign of God's sheer power and control, as well as His generosity. Today, the creationist view of the universe is almost as heretical as the idea that the sun revolves around the earth once was. In the wake of naturalism, we see the canonical universe shift from caterer to agent of chaos, humankind from everything to nothing. Today, for someone to acknowledge their own *value* as a human being within the universe is little more than wishful thinking under the modern paradigm. We are told that in our religiosity, we have narrowed our view, seeing the universe in a way the materialist would deem grossly simplistic. The Christian may argue that they see the skies for what they really are. The current battle between the perspectives of the cosmos is a symptom of the God argument.

The biblical approach to viewing the stars in the sky returns to submission and humility and a recognition of one's smallness and fragility, without the total loss of self-worth. The natural cosmologist on the other hand disappears into the cosmos while simultaneously conquering it. The former at once recognizes the force and scale of the skies, understanding only in part the mystery of their immensity. Yet they also see the creator of those skies as *more* than the skies. Therefore the skies were meant to be understood only through the lens of creation, and often as a symbol or sign of the relationship or promises between God and humanity. God led Abraham outside to show him the stars as a vast symbol of an individual promise—a promise that would change the course of history. God made the skies as unsearchable and unreachable, as dark and light, as visible and invisible as the human heart. His intentionality in the design of both ought to be recognized, and the subsequent implications considered. The recognition and implications of such a link between creature and creation leads to a hope of evolving knowledge and discovery, as well as a humble concession to an eternal and unsolvable mystery.

The two different views of the skies represent an opposition of worldviews. If we cannot agree on something as high as the sky, how can we agree on something as low as humanity's formation from the dust of the earth? The great unknown void between each star can be as great as the chasm between two high minded opinions. Light becomes the only thing capable of crossing that distance. The distinction between attitudes can be traced to the beginning, as well as similarity. The skeptic and the believer agree that in the beginning there wasn't anything, and then suddenly there was everything. All matter and space came to exist in time. The discrepancy is in how one considers the *nature* of the beginning. Will we face the question of universal origin from a tower of thought that has been built to have dominion over the skies, or by humility and submission to their mystery and origin? Regardless of where we stand on this question—as ignorant stargazer or brilliant cosmologist—we can agree on one thing: we are dust. Whether we were formed by the dust of the stars or the dust of the earth is up for debate. To one, we are the dust of the stars, and to the other, we are the dust of the earth. Which perspective stands more prominent as true *divinity* depends on the winds of the science and culture of the times. Our home is either naturally built among the stars or on the earth. Humankind will always attribute its existence and emergence from one of these places, placing the hope of the true home either here on earth or on some distant planet.

The beginning of the Bible first tells this tale of the collision between the different cosmological viewpoints. It is apparent that humankind's endless desire for cosmic intellectual conquest did not emerge in the twentieth-century space race. The desire to know the *truth* about our beginning began at the beginning. The first desire to know all things resulted in man and woman reaching up and plucking their desire for knowledge from its tree. The world was indeed flooded with knowledge—and water. After the waters of God's judgment receded, the first tower to the heavens was built, that humans might again know everything that God knew. In order to realize our thirst for knowledge, we must first acknowledge the truth that it is a thirst we've had all along, a thirst that only exists on the everlasting shore of withdrawing waters.

Humankind still desires to move upward against nature and gravity. But nature and gravity have always forced us back down to the ground, doomed to scratch our heads in perplexity. We can move upward in one of two ways. Either we will force ourselves upward in rocket ships, or we will be given a hand up when we recognize the benefits of humility. The Tower of Babel, while I believe it to be true, is also a potent metaphor for the current debate that situates itself in the void of space. The search for answers must work its way from the ground up. It cannot start from the tyranny of the stars. The Bible provides us with a starting point: in the beginning, God created the heavens and the earth—the closest things we know to infinity. One cannot know the nature of infinity and beyond until one understands what resides within oneself—namely an infinite tendency for evil beyond what we're able to understand or willing to admit. If we know we are lowly, *made* from the dust of the earth, we may seek to know the one who made us. Otherwise, we will always be searching for the way in which nothing piled us up from nothing, eventually turning us into animate mud castles of chaotic space-time. The nothing theory could cause those made from the dust of the stars to simultaneously contemplate their own divinity and meaninglessness. In other words, natural cosmology makes human nature itself a stark contradiction, wherein we are little more than microbes and nothing less than our own gods.

The contradiction simply cannot be solved through math, science, or astrophysics. There is too much *dark energy* moving behind the scenes. There is no shortage of pride in the universe, a pride which blinds us to the contradiction. No matter how many times humans gaze upward and outward, they will always be forced to look back downward and inward, by way of the metaphysical equivalent of Newton's gravitational laws. After all, we must stop and tie our shoes every once in a while even in our most epic journeys. The beginning and the farthest reaches of space are as invisible to us as the force that causes apples to fall from trees. Both theist and theorist know that there are invisible laws; they exist as both facts and mysteries without their factual nature cancelling out their mystery or vice-versa. The theist tries to avoid the realms of total theory by acknowledging mystery, as the theorist avoids theism to convince himself that he has overcome the mystery with facts, even if those facts are only fudge factors—which are often intellectual greasepaints to hide the uninterrupted fact of mystery.

An aspect of these laws is very human, as are the ways in which the laws are perceived either as malleable or fixed. It seems that their design has evolved alongside our history in the cosmological view. They can be invented, hypothesized, poked at with space needles, theorized, explored, experimented on, presupposed, and in some cases shattered on the ground in frustration and traded for a new theory. In the end, humankind finds its greatest insights from its humblest observations. One will likely understand the *true nature* of a frog more by watching the way it acts in nature than by dissecting it and examining its organs under a microscope. The same principle goes for much that is and was, and was from the beginning. Many stones may have been best kept unturned. The apple of Newton was destined to fall, but the apple of Adam ought to have stayed where it was.

The end of humankind's search for the pinnacle of knowledge is indeed in the religion of evolution and the cult of cosmogony. Perhaps these answers exist and will one day be found cleverly compiled by a black hole in the farthest reaches of space-time, or written concisely in a library within the smallest subatomic particle. The question is, what then? Either we will become as gods or we will return to the dust as mortals (or be crushed within the event horizon).

I love lying on my back and enjoying the stars. The stars tell both of eternity and of humanity, finite beings existing in what we comprehend to be the mystery of the infinite. The stars were there watching throughout many great battles and the rise and fall of nations. Today, we are told that the presence of the stars indicates only the absence of their creator. There are things I will likely never know about the stars, including exactly how many there are. Why then would I presume to know that it is right to doubt the one who is behind even the stars that I cannot see but am forced to believe are surely there?

LA VIDA LOCA

M<small>Y VERSION OF THE SCIENTIFIC</small> definition of life is "the processes by which any type of organism begins to exist apart from its parent cells or organisms." I think that a far simpler word can more succinctly describe the many facets of life—being. Being simultaneously describes mind, body, spirit, and essence—and it is a word that causes much controversy in our modern culture because it ascribes innate value to every individual, which up to this point cannot be automatically inferred without to some degree conceding to the invisible and the mystery. This value, like the very laws by which the universe is governed, cannot be adequately tested and repeated by the modern scientific viewpoint, so value of life itself in a sense becomes void. However, like the origins of the universe and the origin of language, the origin of human and animal is original— the natural philosophy which denies this originality and value is not original. A person is not a cosmic cliché, even if he or she randomly stumbles across their prescribed words and slogans to defend the mundaneness of life. Just as the universe can be traced back to its logical beginning, so can the individual. The materialist cries out to complicate these beginnings, and to set upon them a stifling weight of indiscernible factors, all in a tireless crusade to indefinitely blur the obvious reality of life's innate value by shamelessly seeking the mindless processes by which the beginnings came about. When the definition of life and beginning are undermined for the sake of scientific progression under atheistic presuppositions, there are major metaphysical, moral, and philosophical implications and ramifications—an annoying empirical fact for atheism that needs repeating. There is no longer a belief in the sanctity of life, and our origins melt into pond-like fables about beginning that denude life of its truer essence. The struggle and battle for freedom from the perceptual dogmatism of the *value of being* has placed humankind into a new type of bondage. Rather than choosing whether or not to keep the laws of God, humankind has chosen to keep only the law of itself. The dichotomy of knowledge again signifies a battle of worldviews, illustrated earlier by the divergent attitudes of Aristotle and King Solomon toward humanity's ongoing quest for wisdom—whether it be worldly wisdom or godly wisdom: "The fear of the Lord is the beginning of understanding" (Proverbs 9:10); "Knowing yourself is the beginning of all wisdom" (Aristotle). When our definition of life becomes more materialistic and less rooted in our God-given value, life itself becomes cruel and imperialistic, for we tyrannize ourselves by our faulty knowledge of who or what we are. A living person becomes less of a being and more of an organism, and can be dealt with as such as members of a society, as history has shown.

As the times change and we become more "sensible," organic humanity transitions from a creature with sanctity and value into a *next to nothing,* cosmic accident. A being and a creature had a beginning, but like the desired endlessness of the uncreated and purposeless universe of atheism, the organic man and woman never really began—it would have been impossible to place a concrete definition even on a word as simple and primordial as beginning, without also endlessly breaking it down into its smaller parts. For a beginning assures us of purpose, parameters, direction, and intentionality, just like the exposition of a written story, making it impossible for the interpreters of the beginning to simultaneously be the authors of the beginning, often to their frustration. In order to change the authorship of existence, one must wage war with the very meaning of existence itself. Our existence becomes only bacterial. After all, if we all evolved from the same single-celled organism, how can we legitimately or logically ascribe any more value to our being than the algae from which being itself came? It would only be a relativistic determination of human value, which is what we see. Our origins can be traced back to the infinitely small, infinitely unknown, and the infinite unconsciousness of science, whatever that may mean at any given time. It is from this infinity that we become divine authors who are enslaved to meaninglessness, the trade-off we took when we chose to become as gods. Therefore, in a world stripped of the invisible, only we have the right to justify the subjective placement of more or less relative value on another individual's being, often depending on how that placement of value may suit our own survival at any given time or in any given circumstance. "Have you not made distinctions among yourselves, and become judges with evil motives?" (James 2:4; *I am aware this is not the correct context of this verse*).

The fight between science and religion is actually a battle between two entities that ought to shake hands and have a good conversation, but it has become much more like a holy war between two religions. One religion calls the beginning of life and the universe Genesis 1, and methodological naturalism calls it the big bang theory, even though this cannot even be adequately pinned down as the definitive beginning of everything any more than some vague concept of an amoeba can be pinned down as the definitive beginning of life on earth. Many in the first category cry out to God with a humble thankfulness concerning life, believing that He knit them together in their mother's womb, while many in the latter category support senseless things such as abortion, slandering and deriding those who believe in the inherent value and mystery of being—a value which is also codified in life's *scientific* definition of beginning, new life having been formed in its first few cells. Make no mistake, the undermining of the innate, inherent, and invisible value given to us by God—which by nature exists apart from a natural philosopher's relativistic definition—will end in the ultimate destruction of the sanctity of human life by means of systematically eradicating all standing objective moral values, if it hasn't already.

Jesus Christ proclaimed that He is the way, the truth, and *the life*. He simultaneously is the essence and definition of life for the Christian. The Christian understands that life is essential and clearly defined. Therefore, human life has a value that cannot be stripped of its definition based on the whims of the world, because it was not primarily defined by humanity. No individual or society has the right to jeopardize the inherent and incalculable value of other individuals or societies based on subjective distinctions. Man is not his own maker, nor woman hers. The apostle Paul states that the mind of sinful man is death. Christ states that if a person denies Him, who is life, they will die in their sins. The message of Christ is simple, but it is in agreement with science. Life has its beginning in essence first and foremost, and death is the absence thereof. However, Christ did not say, "So far, I have the best definition of life," but rather *"I am the life."* In the statement "I am the life," Christ hereby states that He exists with the very same name as the God of His earthly fathers, the God who was known to give life to all. His existence is the answer to our search for a concrete definition of life that does not discredit an essence apart from the material. If we reject Christ's definition and self-description, He tells us we reject the most fundamental component of life—which is God. When we reject His image, we end up forgetting our own. This is where the disintegration of the individual and social spirit begins.

In our nation, and indeed our world, the notion of God as foundational or even beneficial is undoubtedly being scrutinized. This notion is on route to being destroyed as efficiently as possible. All things consist in Christ. This assertion operates under two guiding statements, one of fact and the other of belief. If true, its implications are foundation changing and ought to scare us back into our wits. The *fact* is that all things do indeed consist. If all things did not consist, there would not be any consistency in any one thing, like a sunset or the taste of coffee. The sun would burn out, the moon would crash into the earth, and you and I would become convenient little molecular ash piles. The *belief* is that Jesus Christ is the reason for the consistency of all things—things that are, things that were, and things that will be. This verse tells that Christ is one with God, who created all things and holds all things together, assuming that people back then knew that all things are being held together by someone. The more one comes to know Christ, the more His identity as God becomes as apparent as the visible facts behind what consists. If He holds together all things, then He also holds fast to the definition and true meaning of life. Yet, as we see in postmodern culture, the definition of Christ, along with all notions of definition, are being systematically stripped away. The definition of truth becomes as it was for Pilot, the denial of its definition. For the material person who came from nothing as a cosmic accident, the only truth can only be truth's ultimate absence. When we see these ideas permeate our culture we can suspect—especially in the wake of the bloodiest century known to humanity—that they may lead to nihilism and unprecedented atrocity. Christ is not only the definition of life; He is also the Word who was made flesh, and the light that shines in the darkness. Therefore, the Word, which is traced back to the Greek *logos* (the seat of logic and reason), is also the light which guides away from humanity's chaos, confusion, foolishness and subsequent wickedness. This definition of Christ makes sense of life in its journey from beginning to end. This is indeed the story of the beginning, which doesn't discredit Spirit, the mystery of God's love and the invisible consistency that His love provides which was present at the beginning: "In the beginning was the Word, and the Word was with God, and the Word was God" (John 1:1).

We see what life truly is in this controversy of what life truly is. It is the battle for life itself. It is a battle of words. Rather, it is a battle between centuries of intellectual words and the Word which made the utterance of all the other words possible. To find meaning in inherently true words, we search them out, deconstruct them, and reconstruct them the way we'd prefer them to be. We look into their past, present, and future as if we have omniscience. We examine them under microscopes. The truth of life is in the way in which it can be described, with words. And to understand the meaning of life, like words, we must trace them to their origins. The only reasonable definition of life can be found at the beginning. For the beginning can show life itself as further evidence for God, who is life and who created life—God Himself as evidence for life's sanctity, which is always under attack as an idea. The way in which a person sees their beginning will determine the only reasonable value he or she places on their own life or the life of others. If we exist only as an evolutionary extension of the cosmos, our existence is nothing more than an unlikely addition to matter. Anything outside of what is quantifiable is a myth, and there is no objective reasoning for a metaphysical aspect to humanity. Even consciousness itself can be explained away by chemical "fizzing" in our brains. Love, hate, anger, compassion, and all the array of human emotions connected with the true experiences of life are reduced to their chemical bases of meaninglessness. In essence, they no longer exist. This philosophy can only end in the total cessation of the essential aspects of our humanity, as well as the erasing of both mind and freedom; "They are darkened in their understanding and separated from the life of God because of the ignorance that is in them due to the hardening of their hearts" (Ephesians 4:18). Without true mind or freedom, we are left wondering what else we have in life to cling to. Fortunately, all signs point to the existence of true mind and freedom, even if they won't fit into our test tubes; "In Him was life, and that life was the light of all men" (John 1:4).

In the account of the garden of Eden, God provided Adam and Eve with the definitions of life and death, as represented by two trees. The first tree held the answer to true life, and the second tree promised to erase life. Unfortunately, the latter tree succeeded. The reason human beings *choose* life apart from God is because humanity's sinful desires have stripped God's Word of its authority. The aim of the serpent's first temptation was to destroy God's law. It did this by causing Eve to doubt God's true character, His true life. He asked, "Did God really say?" When a person doubts God as the source of life, they end up doubting life itself, *what* it is or even *if* it can really be. This is a base form of confusion, which today is praised as it's puffed up into modern intellectualism.

BE KIND, PLEASE REWIND

It is typical of our time that it has to look
for its god through a microscope.

—GK Chesterton

A<small>RE WE ORIGINAL OR A</small> cosmic cliché? Methodological naturalism
and Christianity again clash on the subject of origin—surprise,
surprise. There are two different origins that cause this great
controversy. One is the origin of life, the other is the origin of the
universe. Yet no one alive today and engaged in the debate was
actually around to witness what the beginning of time and space
looked like. It's an obvious conundrum to remember, yet we forget
it in our pride. A certain level of ignorance in every individual, no
matter how well educated, is as obvious as the orbit of the moon
around the earth. Therefore one should look backward as well as
forward with a little humility. When someone acknowledges that
they actually know less than they claim to know, a good distance
is traveled toward conceding to the countercultural knowledge of
Genesis. At least the beginning of the argument about beginning
has been won by the theist when those who claim total knowledge
over the beginning begin to understand that any beginning cannot
be seen, but can only be believed *by faith* to some degree.

There is another point of agreement. Both faith-based viewpoints
posit an origin, neither of which are infinite. Life and the universe

began at two separate points in methodological naturalism, a singularity and a primordial puddle in a lightning storm, both linked in the same ancient continuum of gradual cosmological change. These two points of origin are billions of years removed from one another. In Genesis, there are also two different origins, but they originated from one original mind as God formed and interacted with matter, shaping nature and life into its Kantian enigma. In Genesis, a conscious agent was necessarily involved to make use out of an otherwise useless environment, much like a lump of clay has little aesthetic value until it is formed into an intelligible shape. For the materialist, time and chance are the only conceivable entities at play as artists. By nature, these have no mind. As a result, we came from mindlessness, we are still in a mindless universe, and we have no minds. I find it slightly ironic that the argument about unintentional origin is argued by people with minds, often to prove the superiority of their own intellect over the theist's. Those who have passionately argued for generations that no mind was present at the beginning, because of the theological implications that the apparent presence of design in nature supposes, often point out that believers, or even those trending toward the mildest skepticism of methodological naturalism, are not using their minds at all when they invoke some transcendent "God of the gaps"—which itself can be a sort of "fill in the gap" insult disguised as an argument to be wielded whenever certain assumptions come under any scrutiny, either by theists or any others who dissent. Yet by the very *nature* of their argument, there can truly be no mind to argue with, for we perpetually exist in relation to and as a result of unintentional origin. There is no basis for argumentation for lack of consciousness, for the conscious existence of a supposedly superior argument about origin collapses in on itself. Argument about an unconscious beginning cannot take place without beginning from intelligence, and reasoning from that foundational intelligence, both of which require consciousness. If the argument is won, the result is purposelessness anyway, so why bother?

In both arguments, there are similarities. At least we can agree on something as simple as "In the beginning there was a beginning." Theists know there was a beginning; their confidence in this has stood unshaken for ages. There was a beginning to all of creation and to us. Atheism also knows that there was a beginning, coming to know of such a beginning much more recently, because the natural signs have caught up to the supernatural ones. Yet this beginning has proven to be problematic for their agenda of promoting the unintelligible exposition of existence. A beginning implies a product, a process, and therefore a producer. The universal fact is that our universe is full of effects, and effects cannot happen without causes. Humanity is caused, although by what exactly is the basis of much disagreement. If we are effects of a cause and thus continuing to cause effects through the daily choices we make, it is likely that some other effect caused us. Was that effect the cause of a choice, or of random chance? What cause caused that effect, and by what choice or lack thereof (and back on into infinity, or so we're told)? Naturalism by name can look backward only within its self-limiting nature as an effect of a cause. Part of the answer to beginning can be observed in the finitude of all things and is exemplified in the bodily mortality of human beings. Anything finite must be caused, as mortal humans are caused. These effects by their finite nature illustrate an initial uncaused cause, and an inference to the best explanation—especially realizing our limitations in concretely rediscovering beginning without a time machine—would logically suppose the uncaused cause of everything finite to be infinite. Whatever is finite must have both beginning and end by definition. An infinite regression of finite causes becomes oxymoronic to any honest human after too long, for no matter how much we evade the upcoming presence of a clear and conscientious choice which existed outside of this finite regression, it will show up at the end, which is the beginning. However, this conclusion does not alone prove that the God of the Bible is that initial cause. It simply implies that an initial uncaused cause is likely and that it is likely a result of choice, which indicates agency. Once we recognize the presence of choice outside our sphere, we may reflect on both the most likely attributes of and the most likely candidates for that decision maker in order to help close the intellectual gap as far as identity is concerned, even if it is unlikely that this gap between human knowledge and what transcends it will be closed strictly via intellect.

We can't help as humans but to scratch our heads as we think about who or what caused all things, including ourselves. It may be one of the wisest things to throw our hands up and admit the impossibility of a rock solid conclusion, a "theory of everything" that comes of our own volition to once and for all take the place of God, bringing us to an end without revelation.

A question we must ask ourselves to help further narrow this intellectual chasm is whether any other deity, deities, or natural phenomena fulfill the criteria of the choice maker in the same way as the God of the Bible. Why must He be the primary cause? Let's examine a few other candidates to see how they stack up.

Another type of monotheistic God invoked to explain this cause is a deist god; that is, a god who started the universe and then left it to its own fate, to govern itself while he went on eternal vacation to the Bahamas, thus not being too concerned with whether or not I capitalize his name. This god is not a blind watchmaker, but an indifferent one who formed everything, washed his hands clean of divine responsibility and stepped away. He now is far too busy to worry about our universe. Those who believe in the deist god also have a convenient out pertaining to their behavior and adherence to any moral law, if this god even has one— in other words there is no serious objective basis for ethical accountability, but there is the benefit of believing in a god if and when it's expedient to do so, or denying god's authority or agency when that's advantageous. Therefore, how can deism conclusively make moral claims without the same backdrop of relativism as atheism?

Let's examine whether this god fits our common sense, whether or not he or she fits our common convenience to be cosmically absolved of moral responsibility. Everything from the basic building blocks of life and matter to the grand scale of the skies is undeniably *consistent*. They continue to operate in a similar way as they always have. One who denies this pattern likely will not deny tonight's sunset. In the New Testament, this consistency is said to be held together by Jesus Christ Himself. The way nature operates, from the lights in the sky interacting to the human patterns of autonomy and anatomy, indicates consistency, which designates the continuing presence of the source of that consistency. Romans 1 tells us that the signs in nature, or creation, indicate a *specific* God—that is, one who has been present and not absent throughout history. Let's face it. If God created everything with such stunning accuracy, meticulous thought, and the absolute presence implied in His creativity, is it even logical to assume that He would simply step away from everything? Common sense says no, and God intended it to. Everything in creation points to the existence of God. It also points to the character and *presence* of God. The *nature* of nature in its consistency is inconsistent with an indifferent god. Think about humanity's desire for fellowship, love, beauty, and so forth. The nature of creation undeniably reflects our own faculties to marvel at creation and try to comprehend its nature. In the same way, the sheer immensity of all that is also reflects who God ultimately is retrospectively on a much smaller scale. How dare we anthropomorphize all the good things that we see as symptomatic of ourselves as we label Almighty God as cold and as indifferent as Pluto. Deism is only a perceived transcendence of the human imagination with the convenient intention of total ethical independence.

Another supposed cause is the idea of pantheism, multiple gods, or God as a little bit of everything to be found in anything. For example, the Hindu religion has millions of gods. This religion can be found throughout many different cultures. The basic idea that there are separate gods in control of separate elements or attitudes, or within all elements and attitudes, is an old one. Many other ancient cultures like Greece and Rome also used the concept of many gods or God in everything to explain the intelligible and consistent patterns in nature. There may be a god of the sea like Poseidon, who is turbulent or calm based on his mood, of lighting like Zeus, or of Hades in the underworld, and so on. Many of these gods seem to hold the same cold, pitiless indifference to humanity as the deist god. These are gods that are terribly inconsistent with one another, and often seem only to reenact human fallibility on a cosmic scale. The Greek gods were always at war with one another, at times engaging in atrocities like cannibalism or ravaging human women. These tendencies show mythologized abjection, not true divinity. They were always committing violent and heinous acts that made no sense, even from a human standpoint of justice. They simply made an exciting story.

Think of it this way. Right now as you are reading this, you are breathing air, hopefully. Perhaps you woke up next to your loving husband or wife. You may have little children running around the house. You may have a fridge full of food and a faucet with cold or hot water on demand—of course there are many without these basic amenities, of whom Christ calls blessed. All these things and many more were made possible somehow. The existence of love, the information needed to build life, the abundance of air and water, and much, much more do not seem to indicate the design of a group of often ruthless, violent, and indifferent gods. Of course, there are negatives in creation like sickness, poverty, world decay, and death. But the fact that you are alive within the conditions that you are in is astronomically unlikely, even if you've been told the opposite and even if you feel consistently "normal" from day to day. This normalcy depends on consistency, which is incredibly inconsistent with an abnormal, chaotic existence. The mythological pantheistic war-gods are not the ones to thank for this undeniable abundance and unlikely existence of ours.

The third option of how things came to be is by strictly natural phenomenon. I think this is the easiest mistake to clear away, yet is the most prevalent in the modern paradigm. It is the popular stance of science, as it is defined in modern terms, with its ultimate anti-teleological aim to discredit anything resembling faith-based thinking. Many incredible scientific minds of the past have admitted humbly and with joy that there is and will always be an invisible element of mystery hidden in nature, behind the processes we can observe and test. Today, methodological naturalism prides itself on pursuing the knowledge of everything, especially origin, and purging the world of all sense of awe and mystery in a frantic denial that there are some things that will not be known.

To conclude that all of life and existence and everything that is came into existence by the irrefutable absence of mind is truly a hard pill to swallow. How could consciousness emerge from the unconscious, material from immaterial, and the physical from the ethereal without the presence of a great and powerful mind to direct—one who is capable of placing immense stars in the sky and thoroughly coding who we are into the tiniest systems imaginable? It is impossible, or at the very least astronomically improbable, for utter disorder and chaos to create uniformity and complexity, let alone apparently limitless uniformity and complexity. Quite simply, from nothing comes nothing.

From a materialistic point of view, effects must be traced back through their causes—and the presence or absence of choice ought to be determined. When we see that something is caused, we do not assume that nothing caused it. The same principle ought to exist for the skies above us and ground below. The universe exists. At one point, it came into existence. Therefore, it has a cause. Since this cause cannot be explained through observation, one ought to consider all given factors in order to make an inference to the best explanation. To observe a chain of causation and attempt to trace it back to its logical beginning, as far as we know, is impossible, for we have no absolute capabilities to do anything other than theorize explanations for such things. No matter how one regards the beginning, as indicative of the strictly natural or the transcendent, some element of faith must be used to explain it. If the chain of finite causes and effects was infinite, there would be no beginning, no ultimate or transcendent cause, and no final period at the end of the sentence to once and for all answer the original question. The infinite regression of finite causation strikes many as an adequate answer for a finite beginning, but is a contradiction in terms which eludes the real questions that arise as a result of the apparent agency involved in the creative process, inferred by what we observe day to day. This infinite regression was popular among some who cultivated a natural view of all things because it seemed to back the philosophical presuppositions of naturalism—Albert Einstein, for example. It simply eliminated a need to invoke God to explain the way things are. In the eyes of those who do not presently want to deal with any theological implications of the sciences, God is the ultimate fudge factor, and an unacceptable explanation for the unexplainable. However, in erasing God from origin, theorists have had to invoke all sorts of new and less likely cosmological and biochemical fudge factors. In so many words, the God of light was traded for dark energy.

Theorists and cosmologists with atheistic presuppositions had long hoped for the general stasis of the skies, infinity in time and space to prove the infinite regression. But even their experiments illustrated finitude in both time and space, big bang cosmology itself indicating finitude, an unwanted beginning of the universe. The universe was found to contract into the past until it was at its single smallest point, nothing more than a thought. An infinite singularity of incredibly dense and unlimited potential was theorized to escape the dreaded and archaic *Word*, which so far had sufficed for many. Alas, all things could come into being, without the existence of a being to bring them about. All that is now was once held in the bondage of the purely insentient potential of time, space and life. The Word was finally able to exist apart from someone that could speak it. Potential of the matter within a formed thing alone is rarely an adequate explanation for why or how the thing came to be formed in the first place, as the potential does not rest in the matter of what is formed, but in the one who forms the matter.

There was indeed a singular initial cause for the universe that is posited by modern cosmologists. The universe apparently is observably finite. Therefore, nothing infinite can exist therein, and by nature, the universe must itself be finite. The next step in the wake of acknowledging the beginning of space and time would have to be to ask if this beginning was directed or undirected—with a type of potential, whether likely or unlikely, necessitating each alternative beginning. Was an invisible and mindless potential of what could be alone enough to explain the primary cause? Or was the universe itself secondary, a reflection of unlimited brilliance, creativity, time, and power? Such a transference of conscious potential into unconscious potential is only a last ditch effort to diminish the nagging intentionality present in the beginning.

Such an effort is analogous to attributing life and movement to mirrors or art, which by their nature can only reflect or mimic life and movement. When a person looks in a mirror, they see themselves as they are. But the mirror reflection is lifeless and cannot exist apart from the living person who stares into it—thus the potential of the mirror to show life is not in the mirror but in the one who stands across from it. Likewise, art is a result of creativity and sometimes can be explained and interpreted differently than was intended by the artist, even contrary to its intended interpretation. But the potential of art to evoke certain responses, emotions, or interpretations (even if they are entirely incorrect) did not emerge from the matter that constitutes the art alone. Great works of art and literature can sometimes seem immortal and to take on a life of their own, but such a display is only a residue of the life within the artist or author. Such works could not have existed without their creators' potential or mindfulness. Rather than clone the self, the artist expresses the self. Only then can the *specific* traits pertaining to the artist's identity and the way they see the world be *observed* in their art, although the artist cannot be fully known through observing their art.

The Bible says the same thing about creation itself that a work of art says about its artist—namely that the artist exists, or existed. If the universe was caused, which is implied by the evidence for the finite universe and its beginning, then that cause must have occurred from an outside source. Something or someone must have transcended time and space as we know them.

The philosophical ultimatum lies at the heart of the intellectual battle and permeates the scientific community, and it is actually this ultimatum that points toward the God of the Bible, and Christ in specific—for a clear and present choice of the path we choose has been present since the beginning.

In all known experience, there is only one thing that nothing has been known to produce—nothing. However, our senses may deceive us, for the human definition of nothing implies something apart from what can be known by the senses—it is that which does not exist. But is the invisible nothing by means of its invisibility? Secondarily, would something which transcends time and space as we can comprehend them in our finitude be more likely visible or invisible to the human eye? The God as nothing argument cannot be proven solely based on our inability to see God—just like there are certain soundwaves that cannot be perceived by the human ear. Although soundwaves (or light particles as the visual equivalent) are not a direct analogy, as soundwaves do not by nature transcend the way we experience reality, they do show that there are obvious limitations of the human faculties to see and hear even quantifiable things. Perhaps these limitations "transcend" hearing and eyesight, and enter into the realm of perception.

Naturalism states, if something is material and quantifiable, then it is indeed something after all. However, the science and knowledge of the times both point to the undeniable *existence* of this so-called nothing which replaces God. We are told that there are immaterial components that cannot ever be seen or fully understood that caused the existence and relation of all material bodies in the known universe, from the smallest particles to gas giants. Based on the scientific argument of everything coming from nothing alone, a reaffirmation of the teleological harmony between the seen and the unseen can be reasonably inferred. This reaffirmation maintains major metaphysical insinuations that beg a response from every individual to make reasonable conclusions about what is known. The question is, does the harmony of the unknown maintain to the farthest reaches of space and time? Methodological materialism is largely the practice of finding a way to avoid the implications of this harmony no matter the monetary or intellectual cost. The continual practice of avoiding the unavoidable ultimately points to the existence of what can no longer be avoided, that is a transcendent being outside of what is observable. There is a harmony between wind and water, mind and body that holds true throughout the known universe. *Laws of nature* are contradictory without both body and mind, signifying order. For just as from nothing comes nothing, from chaos can only come disorder. This shows that the God who created everything must value both what is visible and what is invisible. He does not desire to do away with body or mind. And in Christ, God took the very finite and mortal form of man, indicating how important He thought we were, both body and soul. This is further indicated by many of His teachings. For example, Christ told His listeners not to fear those who threaten to kill the body, but He who can kill the body and send the soul to hell. This idea shows God's authority over the physical and metaphysical being. Also, in Christian theology, the culmination of God's judgment on the earth does not result in the total erasure of the physical universe for an ethereal existence but rather promises the restoration of everything to the way it ought to be. Science cannot be all material or it would not be science any more than it can be all philosophy. How could breakthroughs in scientific thought be achieved without consciousness and, dare I say, humility? The understanding of a thing and the thing itself are not materially linked, and for understanding to take place, there is by nature an immaterial process in thought.

As conscious beings, humans are both physical and metaphysical. We cannot escape the relationship between the two. Although the brain exists materially, the function of mind cannot be explained purely by chemical processes. Consciousness arises from the brain and simultaneously exists apart from it. Take a computer as an illustration. The computer alone is not capable of operating apart from an active agent, the computer operator. Our brains are designed to perform many unconscious functions, but it alone as an organ cannot intentionally function without the presence of mind—the analogical equivalent of a college student behind the screen typing his or her thoughts into essay form. This small illustration of the brain and consciousness, and the smaller picture of a computer and its operator, are symptomatic of a much larger reality concerning the relationship between the physical and metaphysical.

The typed college essay shows that both a computer and its operator were functioning in sync to create the final product. Our brains are to our bodily viability as our minds are to our being. All human history and thought shows the symbiosis of mind and matter. The fact that these things exist within a material universe shows that the universe itself is at once material and a *product* of mind. The inner workings of the universe and the striking unlikeliness of our existence therein increasingly demonstrate a functional system exponentially more complex than our brains, even as our brains are much more complex than a computer, and a computer much more complex than a blueprint for that computer, and so on.

I argue that the mind exists as a separate entity from the brain, as the mind is connected to the entire being, whereas the brain is only an extension of the organism. The brain and its functions are observable to a certain degree, but the majority of the operations of the mind remain unseen. For example, when viewing the brain through a scanner as it reacts to stimuli, one may see which areas of the brain are being stimulated, such as fear, sadness, and critical thinking. But this is quite a limited insight into the complexities of the human mind. If one were trying to understand the operation of thought, one would do better to observe a piece of writing from that person, or a piece of artwork, or engage with them in conversation than to observe the physical and chemical reactions of their brain through a scanner. Although by speaking to the person or reading what they write, they will not be able to see inside the physical brain, they will have much better insight into the mind of that person.

This is analogous to the way in which we view life, the universe, and the origin thereof. We can dissect them or observe the way they are, drawing conclusions from those observations. Theories and facts are not designed and posited by solely observing material things and realizing that they exist but by also realizing the *nature* of that thing, whether living or not. One must observe what caused the thing and how it reacts relationally with other things around it, and upon observation make a judgment about that thing's nature. We know more about our universe now than we did one hundred years ago. One hundred years ago, we knew more about it than one hundred years before that, and on and on. Part of the reason for this is because of what we have seen. A much larger reason is what we have not seen but theorized. The principles of all the things that keep our planet spinning around the sun are based on highly sophisticated mathematics as well as imaginative theory. Gravity is the invisible yet unconquerable idea that posits itself as likely the most prominent condition for the origin and continued existence of life. The way we have come to our most modern sense of existence in this universe is itself based primarily on theoretical principles.

The harmony between invisible and visible, mind and body, creation and its nature, divinity and humanity can be found in the person of Jesus Christ. John 1 explains, "In the beginning was the Word, and the Word was with God, and the Word was God ... Without Him nothing was made that has been made." In figuring what kind of God is necessary to meet the criteria of the universe and what kind of authority His words carry, one would do well to look first at the first Word mentioned as being with Him in the beginning, by which he made everything (including the universe). Therefore, the beginning cause had at least two elements that were at the same time one, God's being (His presence and existence) and His Word—signifying unity of potential and intelligence. God the Father and Jesus, His Son, are one, yet both are distinguishable from the other. They operated together, the Bible says, as an agent of unimaginable intellect and power in order to provide us with our *origin*. They were and are both informative and active, operating within the visible and invisible realms. Yet Jesus reminds His disciples that He and the Father are *one*. The controversy over the Trinity faintly reminds us of the current controversy over the existence of consciousness, but on a divine scale. How can mind and body both exist separately and as one? One is informative, and one is active, one material and one immaterial, yet both act together as one, and neither one negates the other.

The quickest and most convenient way to express ourselves is by our words. In a way, our words become us. Proverbs 15:4 says, "The tongue that brings healing is a tree of life, but a deceitful tongue crushes the spirit." The relation of the tongue to the world and people around it, whether it crushes or heals, is not scientifically quantifiable, but it is very real. "But no man can tame the tongue. It is a restless evil, full of deadly poison" (James 3:8). We see this law at work around us every day. The world pattern largely is the way it is because of the words spoken between people. The tongue is either an agent of peace or destruction, often manifesting physically into relationships or quarrels. God created everything by His Word. "In the beginning was the Word, and the Word was with God, and the Word was God" (John 1:1). When we consider the various impacts of our own words, many of which are uttered in ignorance, we may also consider what the divine Word may have been capable of producing in His infinite power and wisdom.

Jesus healed illnesses, cast out demons, changed the weather, and created and unified nations with His words. Men and kings ravage continents and oppress the vulnerable by the power of their words. This reality eludes the origin myth of natural selection acting on random mutation. Words are the basis of all that is built, labeled, measured, and related. They are the basis of the sciences that we use to guess at our origin. They are the way we communicate and thus *evolve.* Buildings are built by words. Words are given through thought. Those buildings therefore must have been immaterial before they became material. The glory of the end product indicates the wisdom of its architect: "The wise woman builds her house, but with her own hands the foolish one tears hers down" (Proverbs 14:1)

In the beginning, God created everything that is through the power and authority of His Word, by the power of intelligent agency. The Word is found as John's primary identity for Jesus. "For by him all things were created: things in heaven and on earth, visible and invisible, whether thrones or powers or rulers or authorities; all things were created by him and for him" (Colossians 1:16). This description ends the search for the harmony between the existence, primacy, necessity, and identity of God. Contrary to what you were taught in school, there was the presence of thoughtfulness at the beginning, and there is still evidence for the invisible attributes of God in the subject of origin, namely His Word. He existed outside time and the universe, and thus before and after them. His power and preeminence indicate that He is the only conscious agent with the means to bring about such an intricate beginning. The Bible gave us the gift of the answer to the current heated debate. It was thousands of years ahead of its time, and still stands strong and unmovable among contemporary hypotheses.

The question of the origin of life on earth falls into the same logical pattern of cause and effect. Besides, the origin of life must also have a primary cause, and this primary cause is often the real battleground of our bloodied worldviews. Isn't it interesting that both questions that most greatly baffle and frustrate scientific naturalists are the questions that by their very *scientific nature* cannot be measured or observed? They would need a time machine for that. Frankly, it appears that God would love to frustrate most the intellectual efforts of those who have been burning the candle at both ends for centuries to try and disprove Him, no matter what theoretical entity they must conjure in order to fill the gaps (directed panspermia and dark matter for example), all while giving people an honest opportunity to choose whether or not to have faith in Him. It is by this means that God offers a superior understanding of things like origin to little children.

NOW BOARDING

The takeoff of a plane is not the reason for a flight, even if it is hopefully the most exciting part. The plane must land at its intended destination, and preferably not in a heap of burning, molten metal. It would be wise to consider our worldview in the same light. Is taking off the only necessary criteria for a successful flight? Will discovering and understanding our origin be enough for us? Will this finally give us the meaning we've been searching for? Thinking about the future can often be more daunting than thinking about the past. Death is the only thing that is universally certain in life, for the materialist and spiritualist, for the believer and unbeliever—yet it is also the most uncertain in another sense. There is simply no escaping the reality that every story comes to an end, no matter how much we forget or train ourselves not to think about the fact. One day, we will all breathe our last breath.

The beginning and the end are both far from our comprehension. In our natural lives, we stand between the two as creatures unable to see either end. This is why every worldview must address destination as well as origin, and each worldview deals with the issue of destination in its own way. Every religion and philosophy, whether natural or ethereal, provides an interpretation. Some philosophies view reality only as an extension of the self. Therefore, in death, we simply recede back inward to our truest form. Some use the idea of reincarnation, which is the cycle of reintegration into different levels of bodily being, based on one's moral achievements or failures: if you gave to the poor, you become an eagle in your next life; if you were a mass murderer, you become an amoeba. For some, we end up in the dirt and return to the dust from which we came. There is no ultimate judgment in any of these views, only a faith spectrum from generation into new life to vanishing into nothing—but this faith spectrum is flawed as it relies on nothing more than human judgement. For some, we blend with the earth, and for some, we blend with the universe. We either overuse our imaginations when thinking about the end or prohibit using them at all. Some will inherit worlds, others will inherit worms, and those who thought they'd found the way will undoubtedly leave behind their clever arguments about that way in order to guide the world to the same place they thought they went. Indeed, we have a vast selection of destinations to choose from, some more convenient than others. But are these destinations equal to one another in scope and truth, regardless of their suitability? Do they respect our humanity or simply diminish it? Are they truly realistic or reductionist? Can they all be true or false? Can one truth stand exclusively or are all inherently equal? Each of these explanations merits some level of faith. We all have faith in what our end will look like. Sometimes we fight wars over it. Only the slain who fought these wars truly know.

I would like to return briefly to the idea of cause and effect. The problem of all that isn't causing all that is was not solved by interpreting the cause of this world, but there it began. If every action or cause has its equal and opposite reaction, no matter how small, wouldn't it be logical to assume that the initial uncreated and eternal action (God's immeasurable creativity) will bring about its equal and opposite reaction (God's immeasurable creation)? The Bible tells us that in the beginning, God was in existence over all things; "The Spirit of God was hovering over the waters" (Genesis 1:1), and that Christ was with God; "In the beginning was the Word, and the Word was with God, and the Word was God" (John 1:1). The Bible gives us many clues to the afterlife, as well as the difference between the manifestation of God's total authority both now and at the end of the age. "In putting everything under him, God left nothing that is not subject to him. Yet at present we do not see everything subject to him" (Hebrews 2:8). Death is not the doorway to a philosophical fairytale; nor is it automatic damnation to eternal nonexistence. Destination for the Christian is a return to life as it ought to be, under the true revelation of the creator's authority. Once again, the Bible is a book of choice, not chance.

Everything we know may be attributed to cause rather than random chance. This cause was brought about by choice, whether good or bad. God chose to create. We chose to rebel. We still stand in relation to the choices made in our origin. And our destination stands before us as a result of our choices. This reality can be seen in everyday choices. The destination of Pizza Hut is reached because of our choice to eat mediocre pizza. It is not the effect of random chance that we end up with either the correct or incorrect toppings on our pizza, but rather choices made on the customer's part and the pizza maker's part. We chose the toppings, and he chose not to listen. That is why he accidently put mushrooms on our pizza instead of onions. Biblical origin and destination are the result of choice and consequence as much as cause and effect. Where cause and effect are matters of matter, choice and consequence are matters of being and agency, as well as our ability or refusal to listen to those with authority. The Spirit who gave us being is the authority above humanity. He tells us the truth about choice—the cause and the effect of choice.

Without consequences, we are free from accountability. We can see how people invent destinations to suit the precept of real, objective accountability and consequence. But this invention often eliminates the presence of choice, and without choice, we are free from the freedom we'd love to see in destiny. Without either choice or accountability, we are free from reason. The conclusion of a godless, purposeless universe and existence can only be the result of the totalitarianism of a cold and indifferent predestination. We become agents of chance only, and therefore, what would be called choice by the reasonable becomes actions by chance for the enlightened. Accountability and responsibility become relative. Although in our sinfulness we may feel life without God to be more autonomous, submission to the cruel, indifferent cosmos actually robs us of any true autonomy we thought we may have had. For whether we turn right or left, kill or love, are rich or poor, we are all under the same conditions, and all of our actions stem from probability, not rationality, morality (immorality), or humanity. We may or may not face human reward or punishment, but anything higher cannot be reasonably expected. With this mind-set, everything that we pretend to choose is actually a result of our actions under the conditions of our immutable evolution, which arose randomly. We are simply in the right place at the right time, or the wrong place at the wrong time. Even Hitler had no choice to destroy a continent and commit genocide; his actions were predetermined via the cruel indifference of *natural* selection—no matter how unnatural it may have seemed to those who fell victim to his more advanced destination theory. Neither was the universe itself a result of choice; it simply became because it had the chance to become. There was no agency or intelligence behind, and thus no choice. In such a universe, we also live without the possibility of agency. Fortunately such an attitude toward life, although modernly in vogue, has always evaded the constitution of common sense.

God chose to make the universe. He chose to make us. At times, one may wonder why God chose to make us *the way that He did*. When we complain about law, we also deny our freedom. We fear that the creator will diminish our autonomy. He doesn't. He augments it when we live in relation to His righteousness through faith.

The skeptic of the law says that God chose to make us without the ability to choose. Therefore, everything human is predetermined because of God's unlimited power and knowledge. It's a powerful argument that craftily evades reason: omnipotent plus omniscient must equal a cruel and domineering master. However, God's power and foreknowledge do not negate His desire to grant us agency. Our everyday experiences disprove the argument that God disbands our freedom to decide our own actions. God endowed each man and woman with the will to choose one thing or another. We do not live in a world system of mindless robots but rather people who show that they are agents of choice, not of chance, despite what they believe. In making conscious choices every day, like the choice to draw unfounded conclusions about God's character, the materialist is consequently revolting against their own predetermined naturalistic worldview, and likewise disproving their theory about the character of God as a cosmic puppet master.

God chose to give every man and woman the opportunity to choose, and every man and woman chooses something. We may even choose not to choose, yet even in this choice, we have also made a choice. There is no escaping the presence of choice. Without the first step in a series of choices, we likely wouldn't make it out of bed each morning. Who we are today is a result of the reality of choice. For example, if the wrong beautiful woman walked past my grandpa, I would not have written this obvious sentence. If my mother chose not to keep me in her womb because of the pressures of this world, I would have never written this sentence either. Our world as it stands today is just as much a product of choice as it is a product of our cause, because every cause in relation to being is the product of choice. Every choice is *natural* in that it is caused by our nature, which God chose to allow us to live with although He knew the damage it would cause. The Bible shows a world that perpetually withers as a consequence of the choices of flawed human beings; "The creation was subjected to frustration" (Romans 8:20). Scripture insists that choice indeed can exist, and every choice is dependent on an evaluation and decision of good over evil or evil over good; "When the woman saw that the fruit of the tree was good for food and pleasing to the eye, and also desirable for gaining wisdom, she took some and ate it" (Genesis 3:6). The reason humans can rationalize and justify evil to ourselves, others, and God so well is because we convince ourselves that there is really no distinction between choice and chance; knowledge of good and evil blend together to form a system of self-justification, and thus condemnation. If we get the chance, we will make the choice, and when we make the choice, its consequence must be a result of chance. But God tells Cain the truth about the choices that he makes; "But if you do not do what is right, sin is crouching at your door" (Genesis 4:7). In each decision, there is either a process of personal justification for diminishing moral definition as a result of chance or a humble concession to the reality of choice. Therefore, to say that each choice bears a consequence (or a reward) acknowledges both the aspects of humanity and reality, mind and body, whereas cause and effect only acknowledge matter. Chance is too indifferent to acknowledge anything.

The answer to the end must address both mind and body, and in order to be consistent with reality, it must acknowledge choice. Although our choices in life may bring minor or major consequences, our destination must reveal the culmination of all our lives' choices. My defense for the biblical destination hinges on one simple principle: it doesn't forsake mind, body or the choices made by them. In other words, God doesn't forget about us. The orthodox Christian does not just believe in their soul flying away to a magical spirit land. Nor do we place our faith in a strictly material rebirth, a reincarnation into some arbitrary animal or a new life that is the same as the old one. We base our believed destination on a specific historical event—the resurrection of Jesus Christ's physical body. This resurrection was not just an esoteric idea presented for the spiritual and intellectual elite, shaped and formulated over generations to keep people clouded by false hope. It was an event demonstrated to us by God to prove not only His existence but His identity. The choice of Jesus to lay His life down for His enemies is an illustration of a person who died because of and for our ability to choose. The choice of God to resurrect His own Son is a promise of a similar type of resurrection for all who choose to follow Him as disciples. God the Father and His Son's choices are more eternal than the universe; "Heaven and earth shall pass away, but my word shall not pass away" (Matthew 24:35).

God's promises are eternal, authoritative, and universal. They extend throughout eternity and ring true for every person. The Christian does not desire a departure from their life but life to the full, which is a reconciliation to their creator through Jesus Christ. We long for our minds to be made new by God so that we can live a life for God, who is our creator. This is the way He made Adam. His pattern of desire did not change. Ours did. His will is not inconsistent with the realities of love, choice, and consequence. Ours is. The resurrection of Jesus Christ from the dead is a promise that God does not forsake us or His creation, but will redeem them. This redemption is conditional, and it's waiting.

FOUNDING

Truth is ever to be found in simplicity, and
not the multiplicity and confusion of things.

—Isaac Newton

WELL CONSIDERED CONCLUSIONS, WHETHER PERTAINING to
physical things like science or to metaphysical things like choice,
consequence, and reward, ought to be foundation changing—
especially when reason almost always includes an aspect of the
metaphysical within or surrounding the physical. We can reasonably
conclude by the reality of choice that the mocker is proven wrong
at death. The man that the mocker called a fool for believing the
things of God is proven right, death being a thing independent and
indifferent of their differing IQ levels. If a man sins and does not
believe it is sin, even as he continues to commit his sins in supposed
ignorance, he stands corrected when those sins revisit him either in
this life or after it. If one's natural philosophy leads them to disregard
any claim to rational objective knowledge or absolutes, they cannot
even objectively claim to believe in God's absolute absence—thus
their mocking of the metaphysical is reliant on the fallacious
foundation of having a claim to rational objective knowledge and
an absolute standard of truth to back their claim in the very world
which their philosophy has stripped of such things. As a result of
the implications of things like choice, death, morality, absolutes

and Christ's persistent explanation of these matters, shouldn't we deeply consider the conclusions we come to, and the implications of those conclusions—whether they be scientific absolutism or total mysticism? Jesus Christ indeed suffered and died on the cross and rose from the grave—if such events were disprovable they would have been refuted by now. His existence and identity are therefore authenticated by the authority of His actions, not His philosophy. The modern materialistic wisdom becomes obsolete in the wake of an act of God, for God's actions easily surpass human philosophy, even cumulative human philosophy.

To keep a level playing field, the religious must allow the irreligious the grounds that if certain foundational claims to the faith cannot stand the test of truth, the reason for our faith crumbles, just as a house with no foundation. The earliest church knew this: "And if Christ has not been raised, our preaching is useless and so is your faith" (1 Corinthians 15:14). Christians should be pitied above all others if there was no resurrection. This is important to remember for the believer as well; we must know that the truth on which our beliefs are built still stands strong. If we do not have a firm understanding of what we believe in, we will have built a beautiful-looking home on a foundation of shifting sand. The slightest worldly breeze could blow it over. But if the foundation is built sturdily, it matters not how beautiful the home *appears*; it will be able to weather any worldly condition. Even if an old tent is pegged properly in the ground, it could withstand the storm better than a beautiful mansion with no foundation.

Every person pursues truth differently, but we all hunger for it. Yet the more we go off into sin, the more we want to avoid truth and end up manipulating it, making us more susceptible to believing lies. This is why we hide things about ourselves from others, for fear of sin being found out as we drift further from the life God intended for us. We can hunger for truth as it actually is, or settle for something that appears to be truth. Apparent truth can arise from a number of different practicalities like individual presuppositions, cultural norms, or the opinions of our peers. The fruit of the tree of knowledge appeared to Adam and Eve to contain the substance of a truth superior even to God's, but it was only a deceptive perversion of the truth. This is a stunning allegory for how easily humankind can be deceived by the devil, even today. No person is identical to another, but there is something ongoing and essential in the way humankind both hungers for truth and shields its eyes as it manifests. For belief to exist and thrive, people need their questions answered by God and to question their answers when they are founded on the practicalities of this world. These practicalities aren't eternal, but temporary—which is no solution for our common desire to build an eternal foundation.

The place where we find answers ought to have an authority that is higher than ourselves, our peers, and our culture. It takes no argument to prove that individuals make foolish decisions. We need to look higher than the self. One may say that they must look to the wisdom of their peers, therefore. But even if one's peer is wiser than oneself, that peer still faces the same human condition as the one who goes to them for answers—the condition of the individual need for an eternal foundation. Still others may claim that humanity in its evolving forms of society and culture is the most reasonable entity to turn to for an ultimate foundation. But humanity as a group or society still faces the same issues as the human individual, simply because it only consists of a bunch of human individuals interacting with one another. After World War Two, Nazi leaders claimed that they should not be subject to punishment because they were simply following the *higher laws* of their nation state. Sadly, in a purely evolutionary perspective, there is no reasonable refutation for this argument, even though most people know at their core that it is patently absurd. If there was no higher law than their higher laws, were they really to be expected to behave any differently? This is the dilemma one faces without an eternally sound foundation. The varying sands on which individual, group, and national foundations are built constantly shift, regardless of sheer numbers of people or the popular opinion of the time.

Sometimes our foundational preconceptions may blind us philosophically, materialistically, and morally from the truth. Arguing philosophy with someone who searches for moral answers may not be fitting. Arguing philosophy with someone who is searching for philosophical answers may not work well either if they are using human philosophy as a defense against the truth. The foundation of the truth must be built upon questions that are worth answering. If these foundational answers lead someone philosophically to faith in Christ, it is just as well as if it happened through interest in the topic of morality—for one ought to result in the other. In either case, the chain reaction has initiated with the introduction to truth, leading to the establishment of faith, which is the building of a foundation that triumphs over any human philosophy. "Trust in the Lord with all your heart and lean not on your own understanding; in all of your ways acknowledge Him, and he will make your paths straight" (Proverbs 3:5–6). In each condition, a person will be led from spiritual confusion to spiritual clarity by trusting in and acknowledging the only one who is able to lead them spiritually. This eternal clarification of values requires an authority that is higher than humanity's temporary opinions.

If our entire worldview hinges on our own perception or on the perception of others, it may be fleeting and distorted. It may easily collapse under a relatively small weight, like trial, temptation, or failure in their midst. The most rock solid human argumentation alone for theism in general and Christianity in particular is never enough.

Purely human argumentation for Christianity as "the best option" can always run into the obstacle of pluralism, wherein every idea has its seemingly equal and opposite idea. Each person has an opinion, and God created us all equal. Therefore our precepts ought to be valued no less than anyone else's. When the truth is dwarfed by our own interpretation of it, following Christ becomes simply a nice set of principles to live by, but ultimately no more or less objective than the next person's nice set of principles to live by. Our interpretation of the truth apart from the Spirit of truth makes Christianity as a religion indistinguishable from the world's truth in the eyes of the world. False weights and measures which arise from a faulty foundation create a false sense of equality between ideas and worldviews, and a false sense of security when resting beneath the roof of an inferior idea. Honesty and justice hold true for our perspectives as much as the various prices we pay for better or worse commodities.

"If we are equal, aren't our opinions of what is true equal as well?" one may ask. The answer is *absolutely* in a world where there are no absolutes, and *absolutely not* in a world where there are. The result of a worldview in which differing worldviews all hold equal weight would be total moral relativity and zero accountability or responsibility—in another word, meaninglessness. A societal or personal philosophy will be doomed to eventually collapse with this belief system, like a house of cards, under the weight of eternity. A total equality of worldviews results in the dehumanization of the very people who promote it under the false advertising of unhindered decision-making autonomy in a more or less arbitrary existence. Within such a society of thought, the meaning of life itself can become *equally* valuable and invaluable, crossing between the divine and pathetic depending on what suits the society or individual. Equality of truth in all answers is the destruction of the truth behind any answer, and therefore of meaning.

When one worldview is deconstructed, a new one will be built. This may be for good or evil. When the house of innocence is torn down, a wicked house is built. When the house of wickedness is torn down, an innocent house is built. New and improved philosophies follow in the wake of old, worn-down ones. But the truth, if it is truth objectively, will maintain its structure whether its principles are lived by or not. "When the son of man comes, will he find faith on the earth?" (Luke 18:8). The truth cannot be solely obtained either from individual speculation or popular opinion. If we cannot base our truth on the world or on ourselves, on what may we base it? This book looks at a few different subjects that may or may not be important to anyone at any given time, or the community, based on what that individual or community foundationally believes. In contemplating worldviews, an absolute key to the truth may or may not be found, but is necessary if we are to see things as they are. The area in which one questions is often the area in which they must find answers. "A person finds joy in giving an apt reply; and how good is a timely word!" (Proverbs 15:23). But the area in which one questions may also be the very place where they go to hide from the answer. The answers they are looking for are not answers from God, but from themselves, and are therefore destructive. These answers only feed the sinful desire to reconstruct a truth that has already been deconstructed. Leaning on our own understanding often results in the fruition of fleshly desires, but these desires are bent to our will and not God's. There is a distortion that emerges from a faulty foundation, even if it at first appeared to be solid. Later, we find that we have descended far from reality and retreated further into our sin. Likewise, if we lean on popular opinion for our foundation, we may find ourselves even more lost than if we heeded nothing more than our own individual preference. In short, we need outside, outside help.

Every person who searches and questions God's existence is looking for the right answer, or the right combination of answers. He or she may be looking for answers to why and how God created the universe, or why and how God created the individual, or something of the like. They may be looking for answers for how to solve personal problems like addiction or grumpiness. In each case, the primary question is foundational for each person. In order for God to be proven to them, or at least evident, He must answer their most important questions, though He is not obligated to, especially if our motivations are only for selfish ends or to evade the real answer. Therefore, each body of evidence that is important to someone can be foundational and can carry proof in and of itself, which can translate into many other areas. But at the same time, continuing questions inevitably point to something apart from the long list of objections—something more primary and primeval—especially if that list keeps growing longer and longer and more and more trivial as more and more questions are sufficiently answered. In such cases, the questions are no longer posed to find the answer, but to avoid it at all costs. The ardent critic seems to always have a new impossible hurdle to overcome, no matter how many impossible hurdles they have already overcome. This is not symptomatic of the impossibility of Christianity but of the condition of an individual's disposition towards God. The endless labyrinth of twists and turns in finding a way around the faith begins and ends at the same place. All the problems that we see outside ourselves begin within ourselves. We must remember the real root of the division between criticism and belief.

Many will concede that there probably is a God, but will question whether He may be definitively identified. I usually argue that if He wanted to disclose Himself, He easily could. One may want to impartially glance at historical events to see if He ever did. The Bible more than sufficiently points to the most compelling answer to our long list of questions. It also diagnoses the condition that prevents us from knowing God without God's direct intervention. Thankfully, this condition is universal and inescapable.

The straightforwardness of the Bible, and its claims to foundational exclusivity is often what angers people most about it. Rampant skepticism, criticism, and mockery of anything biblical or worthy of reverence has consisted since long before Christ. If the structure of God's self-authenticating Word is ultimately flimsy and weak, it ought to be torn down with relative ease, especially after many centuries of scientific, intellectual, and historical discovery. But it weathers the ages well. Even in the wake of evolved human reason, the longsuffering and perseverance of the Word ought to be recognized and what that insinuates considered. Does this perseverance make more sense apart from God's presence?

So far, we have looked into the possibility and relevance of God in some important matters. Culture seeks to replace God in virtually all of these matters, but by design these matters cannot be adequately considered apart from God. Do the answers of culture support the full weight of these matters? Do these matters themselves hold the full weight of our eternity? What about the answers we give ourselves? Each person must identify their foundation and see if it is sturdy enough to support what we need, not what we want for the moment. We also ought to look at the context, the life, the teachings, the death, and the resurrection of Jesus objectively. Jesus showed that a meaningful life without God is impossible and that a life lived in stubborn opposition to God is fleeting and undesirable—even if it holds within it temporary pleasures. Jesus also made it impossible to make any sense of His life or our lives apart from a specific, identifiable God.

If Jesus can be refuted, then our faith is futile. But if He can't, and indeed He hasn't, then each person has the most important decision to make in the universe. We can spend our entire lives trying to intellectually connect the dots in order to find the identity of God and to build our foundation from scratch, or we can place our trust in a foundation that is already built. True faith can only be achieved in the latter sense. "See, I lay a stone in Zion, a tested stone, a precious cornerstone for a sure foundation; the one who trusts will never be dismayed" (Isaiah 28:16). Trying to lay this foundation ourselves would be like trying to build a house without a blueprint. A great weakness of a person is to deny their own weakness. By denying our weakness, we only give it more strength over us. Weakness is something present in everyone, and recognition of it is truly rare. It is because of this weakness that we had to build homes in the first place.

ALL THINGS CONSIST

Behold the pattern of the heavens, and
the balances of the divine structure.

—Isaac Newton

Aᴄᴄᴏʀᴅɪɴɢ ᴛᴏ Wɪᴋɪᴘᴇᴅɪᴀ, Cʜʀɪsᴛ ᴡᴀs an ordinary Jewish teacher and religious leader, apparently a leader of some troublesome and undying cult. Some even go as far as to say that He never existed. At least Wikipedia admits He was flesh and blood. Others claim that the information we have about Jesus is limited and difficult to trust. The same is said about the Bible. In other words, everything we know as believers is no more trustworthy than a game of telephone played by a group of six-year-old girls. Yet each attack on Jesus, aside from the attempts to say He never existed, is an attack on His divinity. There is a grand tapestry of skepticism that shrouds any remaining truth about Him. Is there anything reliable that we can still trust today? How do we remove the shroud of doubt that covers the authenticity of the "religious leader" of the Christian faith? The words of Jesus and the impact that He had on all He knew and knows give us insight to who He really is. Even His persecutors admitted, "No one ever spoke the way this man does" (John 7:46).

There is a reason the Bible refers to Jesus as the Word. He is the revelation of God's truth and character to the world. He is the *reason* behind everything we see, as it was by God's spoken word that creation came to be. Jesus is God in the flesh. "He was in the world, and though the world was made through Him, the world did not recognize Him. He came to that which was His own, but His own did not receive Him" (John 1:10–11). When humankind put Jesus on the cross, it demonstrated that its own presuppositions about God were more important than God Himself. Jesus shows us the true inclination of our heart, and it's not good. We are hopelessly warped against God and others. So much so that when we had the chance to, we killed His only begotten Son. Jesus stood in the way of our deepest sinful desire to be our own gods. He contradicted the ambitions of the flesh, the world and the devil. However, Christ's death had to be so in order for God's plan of salvation to be fulfilled, saving even those who were far away from God. When we see Jesus on the tree, we must see that it was our sin that put Him there. We cannot transfer responsibility solely to the barbarism and hypocrisy of the Pharisees or the Romans. But we also must remember that He knew this, which is why He went to the cross willingly, and for all generations. Christ said that He was going to be lifted up, indicating the kind of death He was going to die. He said that His followers would not see Him, and then after a little while, they would see Him again. He was always speaking with authority and full knowledge of humans and God, heaven and earth. His holiness was shown in His works and His words, and so was His humanity. His teachings were shown and verified in His death and resurrection. Indeed, He may be more than a "first-century Jewish teacher."

Skeptics like to point out that the resurrection account appears to be a myth—a reproduction of similar stories. Yet throughout Jesus's life, He was proving His identity at every turn to eyewitnesses, and confusing and frustrating those who couldn't accept the truth. Though His resurrection was possibly the most powerful and important miracle in His life, the stage was set for it. His resurrection showed that He did not only come to show off some miracles for us and then go back to heaven, leaving us to rot in our sinful flesh. He came to share in our humanity and to pave the way for humanity to share in Him. The biblical account of Jesus is heavily slandered and ridiculed. It is discredited all over our world but never disproved. If what the Bible says about Jesus is true, everything in all of creation is secondary to Him, including our own desires. "'As surely as I live,' says the Lord, 'every knee will bow before me; every tongue will confess to God'" (Romans 14:11). Jesus showed His disciples that by God's power, He was given authority over all of nature. "Even the wind and the waves obey Him" (Matthew 8:27). Jesus Christ is much more believable than any of the other mythological characters who had a resurrection. After all, He is the only one who historically existed. Those who saw Him and knew Him made greater claims about His existence. These were not claims based on personal opinion but on mounting evidence and the fulfilling of thousands of years of prophecy. The entire Bible points to the coming messiah. And all the events in Jesus's life indicate that He is this messiah. The writings of John especially indicate His deity. "In the beginning was the Word, and the Word was with God, and the Word was God" (John 1:1); "Before Abraham was born, I Am" (John 8:58); "I am the Alpha and the Omega, the First and the Last, the Beginning and the End" (Revelation 22:13); and much more from these books alone. Jesus claims to be the answer not only to our origin but also our destination. Yet He is not only in those two places, hopelessly apart from us in the here and now; He is here for us here and now. He existed before time and space and will exist after heaven and earth pass away. He entered not only into our sphere but into our suffering on a cosmic and personal scale. The divinity of Jesus tells us two things: God knows precisely who we are in this vast universe, and it is possible to know precisely who God is. "What is man that you are mindful of him?" (Psalms 8:4).

God is not some vague and distant force that we can conjure up in our minds when we're scared or uncomfortable. He eludes our mystical demands and descriptions. He tells us who He is, but we often desire to believe in a God of our own imaginations. God demands that we leave our presuppositions behind and follow Him.

Even in the age of postmodernity and "superior knowledge," there is no need for Him to be told by us who He is. But ever since the earliest age, humankind has made gods in the image of whatever it wants. Today, our philosophies, studies, technology, power, and cultures have muddied in our eyes the true identity of God as Father, Son, and Holy Spirit. We have not stopped making up our own gods. They still fail to come through for us, even though we've found a way to make them glow when plugged into electricity.

If Jesus is as the internet says, just another man with a few reasonable teachings and no true divinity, Christians are to be pitied. We have believed a well-crafted lie for centuries. In fact, we ought to be silently ashamed of ourselves for promoting a doctrine that is blatantly untrue. There can be no meaning behind any of our religion. The ideals and teachings brought forth lack any true substance if they are rooted in deception. In this respect, I can sympathize with those who are upset with Christianity because they think it untrue. Apart from Jesus, it is untrue, fortunately. And apart from His true divine and human nature, all our religiosity is completely pointless. There is no such thing as being born again. There can be no access to the Father. There is no substitutionary sacrifice for our sins. When Paul says we are still in our sins if Jesus didn't rise from the grave, he is aware that there is no difference between the believer and their opposition. Both are equally in darkness apart from the resurrection. Apart from the resurrection, every Christian alive today is living a lie and promoting a false religion. We ought to be pitied and laughed at. Although this seems like an extreme position to take, as if Christianity still has its benefits apart from its lifeblood, the faith was intended to altogether crumble apart from its "first century religious leader."

Christianity cannot exist on life support, by politely tipping our hats to some of its teachings and moral values only as it suits us. The Word of God cannot be dissected, interpreted, or conflated for our own ends. It can only be believed in on the basis of the merits of Christ, which are intricately bound up in His identity. To separate the deity of Jesus from the teachings of the Word would be like separating soul from body. Thus, if these truths about Jesus stand, every man, woman, and child is subject to Him. If Jesus is the Son of God, everything in our reality changes. If we ignore the salvation He provided, we will face the God who created this universe and everything in it unprotected. "It is a fearful thing to fall into the hands of the living God" (Hebrews 10:31). Jesus knew that the Gospel was immensely polarizing. "I did not come to bring peace, but a sword" (Matthew 10:34). The doctrine of salvation is bound up in God's inherent saving nature and our innate peril. The fact that we need to be saved means that we are walking in real spiritual danger every day of our lives, although most of us are unaware of the level of this danger. How often do we see ourselves or our neighbors or family who deny Christ as stumbling toward the slaughter? For my part, not that often. Yet this is what Jesus was teaching. "If you do not believe that I am the one I claim to be, you will indeed die in your sins" (John 8:24).

Every individual must respond to Christ. But it would do us well to remember that everything in the world and in ourselves will be pulling us away from Him. This has always been the case between God and humankind. In Jesus's day, the question of His identity was so deeply polarizing that His opposition crucified Him. It is up to any person to acknowledge this and to connect the universal and theological dots in order to discover whether or not Jesus's identity as the Son of God is authentic. If all existence indicates intent, then we see there is likely a God. If God is all-powerful and outside space and time, we can see that He is likely the eternal cause of our finite existence. If He exists in and of Himself independent of the universe, we should know He has a specific identity. If He has a specific identity and is all-powerful and eternal and designed us with built-in compassion and love, we may deduce that He is not a God who is indifferent to us, just as we aren't (in general) indifferent to others. If these matters remain consistent, He is a God who is able to speak both at once and throughout history continually. If He has spoken to us in our history, He has made Himself known to us, and has made it clear how He did.

Moving from the probability of God's existence to the likeliness of His identity is exactly the line of reasoning the Bible gives. But the Bible gives us more than a provocative and viable option for a God who likely fits the criteria of creator; it introduces us to Him explicitly, so that we are without excuse. The identity of God, Christians claim, was most vulnerably and generously displayed in the man, Jesus Christ. While He was on earth, He passed every test of deity that was prefaced in the prophecies before Him through His words and His works. God, to whom we owe everything, came to us as the life we always seek, rather than the punishment we deserved.

We cannot wrap our human intellect around the full mystery of Christ. Scientifically discovering a thing like the truth of His relationship with the Father is impossible. "No man can come to me unless the Father who sent me draws him" (John 6:44). If a person could come and stake their claim to their divine inheritance through a series of religious or intellectual steps, why wouldn't they? This is what confounded and indeed still troubles the world about Jesus as the one and only way to God. His sacrifice on our behalf reveals our powerlessness to overcome sin. Jesus exists simultaneously as "The way and the truth and the life" (John 14:6). Between material and logical conclusions, there must be an element of faith in the invisible, a step toward the miraculous. But just because faith cannot be explained scientifically doesn't mean it is worthless, or that the invisible God can't manifest to His creation in different ways. Newer scientific theories revolutionize their fields, often to the dismay of their predecessors. Jesus did this to the thoroughly calibrated science of religion, for He is the ultimate manifestation of the invisible God, not the final answer to some anthropomorphic religious equation.

Every person must acknowledge the reality that they, and everyone they know, are headed toward certain spiritual destruction without a savior. "Rescue those being led away to death; hold back those staggering toward slaughter" (Proverbs 24:11); "If you do not believe that I am He, you will indeed die in your sins" (John 8:24); "Unless you repent, you too will all perish" (Luke 13:5). After coming to grips with this and the existence of Jesus, every person must come to a conclusion about who He was and who we are respectively. This question could take years, decades, or a lifetime to answer—but it's worth all the time we have. The less faith is included, the longer it takes to intellectually arrive at the conclusion of the deity of Jesus. Remember, this faith is not only something that must be achieved by us but also an element given to us by God. Once confronted with the reality of Christ's identity and mission, men and women must make the decision to either reject or receive Him. Biblical history and the words of Jesus indicate that He is the Messiah, not only for Jews but for all humankind. It is the stuff of dreams to think that there will be another man who will come and adequately fulfill that role.

The Christian faith was always meant to be shared by being shown. When two disciples asked Jesus where He was staying, He invited them to come with Him and see (John 1:39). Only later would they find that His true dwelling was in His Father's house (Luke 2:49; John 14). Jesus never intended His ministry to be distant. He invited His followers to share His life with Him, even as His body was broken for them to set them free. His message was not only to be grasped by the intellectual and social elite. He dined with tax collectors and sinners. He forgave prostitutes, rebuked hypocrites, and loved and healed the ones you and I might avoid in the streets. He remembered the forgotten, the downtrodden, and the poor. Thus the forgotten, the downtrodden, and the poor were the ones who were most able to see Him for who He truly was. Jesus called to those who were poor in spirit, the lowly, and those invisible to the world as He had been.

There can be no ultimate revelation of Jesus to us without the recognition of our need for Him. We have the tendency to demand that He reveal Himself to us, but we aren't in the position to make demands of God or His Son. Though God is gracious, He is not our servant. He is not liable to answer our questions or to fulfill our visions of Him. To the degree that we understand the reality of the Gospel and what Christ did for us on the cross, we understand that we owe Him everything. This is why Christ still is a stumbling block for so many, just as He was during His time. We are too proud to admit that we are hopelessly lost. "Yet to all who received him, to those who believed in his name, he gave the *right* to become children of God" (John 1:12). Without this right, there can be no further knowledge. A man could not know a woman unless he actually made the commitment to get to know her. Simply observing her from afar and jotting observations and objections about her in his notebook may come across as odd behavior. Why do so many of us approach Jesus in this same way? The best way to know someone is to spend time with them. The same is true for God. There is no one who knows you better than the person who is with you the most. They know your strengths and weaknesses and everything in between. The people who spent the most time with Jesus and knew Him best were convinced that He was the Son of God. The people who know Him best currently are likewise convinced.

If one does not consider this a legitimate claim to Christ's deity, they should remember also that no one has objectively disproven His deity either. Although it is widely thought that this is the case, the reality of the resurrection is historically compelling. The arguments against the history of the cross and the resurrection have become at times rather desperate, like chasing after the wind. They seem as desperate as the simultaneous human desire for *a priori* answers and to avoid the answers we don't like. I find it odd that such great intellectual efforts in our culture are made to discover true meaning, while the one who claimed to universally give it to us is also the only one who is universally dismissed by our culture as absurd, fantastical, or archaic.

I recently watched an interview where a skeptic said the resurrection was only the next in a long line of myths, following after things like Greek gods and demigods who similarly rose from the dead. This attack and similar ones on the Christian faith are meant to create a nebulous of doubt in the believer and the seeker, and to reaffirm the critic in their disposition against the faith. But just like other attacks on the faith, when scrutinized, it does not hold water. Many resurrection "origins" actually are found to follow suit with the Christian one, not the other way around. Upon closer historical examination, they rise in the wake of the true resurrection. They may appear to be more ancient and mystical, but they are just less well known and obviously fabricated.

The biggest challenge to Christianity, and more specifically to Jesus, is all the little criticisms and sucker punches added up together. These create a system of doubt that can seem like an impossible hurdle. The list of objections is as long as the depth of the human heart for continuing in its depravity by creating a long and windy road to nowhere. It is unlikely that one will ever get to the end of this road by meticulously scrutinizing each question, especially as more and more objections with less and less actual substance are piled on by the minute. Such behavior signifies the desperation of the flesh, clinging to whatever stronghold it may. It is unlikely that the minds and hearts of humans will ever run out of objections. I was no different. I also had a deep level of skepticism. My mind was like a doubt-generating machine. But there was a point when I had to say enough and deal with the obviousness of God. As the psalmist says, "My guilt has overwhelmed me like a burden too heavy to bear" (Psalm 38:4). I saw that my intellectual objections did not outweigh my growing need for a savior.

God intended us to have faith in His Son. But if critics keep recklessly objecting to Christianity in order to refute it, we may one day have enough evidence, as we keep finding all the answers, to make faith in the intellectual sense unnecessary. Faith in Christ will simply be proven once and for all, even though the faith of Christ already has been proven once for all. Intellectual knowledge of who God really is may one day be as natural to us as the philosophy of Darwin. Even Christ said, "However, when the Son of Man returns, will he find faith on the earth?" (Luke 18:8).

ASK THY NEIGHBOR

Historians employ a number of common-sense
principles in assessing the strength of a testimony.

—Gary Habermas

Today, we cannot touch Jesus. We cannot see His scars. We cannot cross-examine the firsthand witnesses of His life or hook them to a polygraph machine. Therefore, in ways, we must have a different kind of faith in the 21st century. But our faith is still largely reliant on the accounts of firsthand witnesses. Our faith is strengthened by the testimonies of our predecessors. I've often heard people say that if they saw Christ firsthand, then they would believe; if they saw Him walk on water, or calm the wind and the waves, or heal a man of leprosy it would be enough evidence for them. Then and only then would they would be convinced. But I would argue that this is not always the case. Perhaps they would believe, perhaps they wouldn't. Some do need to witness signs in order to confirm their faith. Lots of contemporaries of Jesus saw many signs, but they reacted to Him in the same way so many of us do today, skeptical of who He was at best and hating Him at worst. Sometimes His miracles only enraged His enemies all the more. Jesus often faced challenges from His opposition. "Show us another miracle," they'd demand. These taunts followed Him all the way to His last breaths on the cross.

The path to faith has not changed, and neither has the human disposition toward the true things of God. The mind-set of humanity still faces the same paralyzing doubt, although this doubt shrouds itself in different forms in different ages. Modernity, self-righteousness, and sensibility are not a new age invention. They cling to every culture.

The writings of the apostles and teachings of Jesus definitely still apply in the twenty-first century. In fact, they have likely never been more relevant than in the century following two world wars and other countless acts of unrestrained evil. These writings are challenging, convicting, disagreeable with human nature, and often times do not align with current cultural norms or standards of political correctness. Worse yet, they often stand directly and glaringly in the way of what we want most in this world. The earliest teachers of the faith, many of whom saw Jesus, demonstrated what the church really is to the world, showing the relation and distinction between the two. The relation and distinction still ought to apply today. There are still Christians who desire to travel perpetually away from sin, and there are those who claim faith and turn a blind eye to the commandments of God, whether for fear of man or selfish ambition. There are Christians who actively recognize their own shortcomings and are constantly battling their selfish nature, and there are those who are blinded by their selfish nature and are falsely convinced they are on the right path. The Christian faith does not change as the Holy Spirit does not change, and as the nature of sin does not change. There will always be two types of teachers, those who offer words of healing, which come through discernment and discipline, and those who give us only what our itching ears want to hear. In America, the church is plagued by a popular and prominent false prosperity gospel. Sometimes these false teachings are overtly noticeable, and other times they sneak in and grab us by the heart. Neither Jesus nor His apostles guaranteed our physical safety or our material prosperity. In fact, they repeatedly show both through their words and their actions that the faith will bring suffering while we are in this world, a suffering which further authenticated the Word. To present a gospel that does away with this important aspect of Christianity is going against the character of Christ and also denying an aspect of our humanity, reducing us to beings that must never deal with anything negative or else we have "lost the victory." In fact, every New Testament book acknowledges suffering as a sign of genuine faith.

Walking freely with the God of the universe does not necessarily mean that we will have a free pass from the challenges of life, but that we will experience suffering alongside Him as He experienced extreme suffering alongside us. As we travel through this life in a world system in which sin and evil are always present, we will constantly be tempted to conform back into its pattern and be torn up spiritually by this conformity, or we may be torn up physically or circumstantially as we travel along the narrow path which leads us away from sin and evil.

Traveling somewhere contrary to this path is a wide road to destruction. It was there at the beginning of the church, promising an easier life and a secret knowledge. The Gnostics infiltrated the early church, presenting their heretical views about Jesus and the faith. Their doctrine was so sneaky that the apostles had to constantly remind the church to be on their guard against it. The Gnostics claimed to truly know the secrets of God. Ironically, one of the secrets was that He cannot be truly known. However, God created humankind out of love and was pleased to show us who He was, from the foolish child to the wise man. He still is pleased to do this. This all is made plain for anyone to see. But even today, there is an argument for a vague and unknowable God. Don't fall for it. God still offers us the opportunity to know Him directly through Jesus. The undying attitude of the Gnostics, which I believe is similar to new age spirituality making its way into the church, is not subject to much change. Although it does take different forms, adapting to new cultures and camouflaging itself so as to be ever more true and relevant.

The church has been plagued by a false prosperity gospel. It has also been plagued by the resistance of modern spirituality. This religion has elements of Gnosticism and is ever changing with the culture, inviting Christian doctrine to adapt to its principles of universality. This is such a large entity and infiltrates so many different worldviews that it cannot be narrowed down to one heretical sect or one religion, yet it saturates much of what we set before our eyes. It is an amalgamation of all the various idols men and women can use to feel fulfilled. Many modern people align new spirituality, scientific theory, and Christian morality to form a religion that they think is less archaic, outdated, dogmatic, and narrow-minded than "fundamental" Christianity. The pressure this puts on Christians both then and now to contradict their convictions is often too difficult to bear. Many have conceded to the more popular view of the times and traded Christ for what the world has to offer.

This chapter was intended to address the importance of the early church in shaping modern Christian thought and life. So far, I have discussed much about the modern church, or rather variations of it. However, I think the modern church, its flaws, and its righteousness fittingly illustrate the character and conflict that was also present in the early church. For the one true church is still alive, as are the churches that war with the one true church, often from within. These types of churches and attitudes are still alive today and have become a prominent source for citing the church's hypocrisy. The emergence of Gnosticism in the earliest churches was symptomatic of a much larger problem that the church has been battling all along, backsliding into the ways of the world. Yet there were always those who stood valiantly and fearlessly against the works of deception and iniquity that arose within the church. The internal battles, dissension, and opposition that the church faces today existed in strikingly similar forms in the first few centuries. This is a sign for what the church really is and what it always was meant to be—both a human and divine *reflection* of Christ on earth.

The humanity and divinity of the character of Christ affirm His identity as the Son of God who was to come into the world. The human and fallible church aspires to follow Him in His divinity, to be disciples. Where we sin, we fail, and where we fail, we sin. The aspiration and struggle of the church to build and maintain her identity as the bride of Christ is evidence in and of itself of the authenticity and true nature of Christianity, and of our tendency to fall short of Christ's expectations. We cannot evade our humanity. The church's history is like a mirror, showing us where we are still flawed collectively and individually. But one thing ought to be remembered: the genuine church, operating under the precepts and doctrine of the apostles and the teachings of Jesus, is not prone to slip from its righteous intent, as long as it maintains Christ as the head. When we as Christians follow our selfish ambitions and try to make others around us agree with what is wrong within the church, we make the church appear hypocritical to outsiders. When we no longer act as agents of love but as agents of self, the image of the church changes in the eyes of the world as much as in our own.

Before Christ, God's chosen people held the spiritual advantage over all others on the earth. This did not mean that they were any more or less human than any other, just that they were the nation chosen by the creator of humanity and therefore had the moral principles that were most relevant to the way in which humanity operates. The Israelites were given many blessings, rituals, laws, and miracles as their nation advanced. Above all, they were given relationship and access to the one true God. But because they were given these things, they were also held at a higher standard. There was more expected of them than the Babylonians or the Egyptians. Their religion was exclusive, and it was extremely difficult for outsiders to practice it or to be granted equality with the Hebrews in the eyes of God. Outsiders either did not have easy access to the knowledge of God because of their geological or social separation from the Jews or when confronted by the God of Israel they were against Him and considered their own gods to be superior.

The clash of nations and ideals continued to manifest for thousands of years until Christ came. At times, Israel and Judah rose up, and other times, they fell, militarily and spiritually—usually hand in hand. There was internal and external turmoil within and among all nations at the times of their rebellion. Nations crumbled from within or were conquered from without, often because of revolt that arose because of the influence of outsiders. If there's one thing history tells us, it's that nations are temporary. The Bible still diagnoses the root of this phenomenon as humankind's sinful and rebellious heart.

Christ came to unite all the nations. He changed the nature of the exclusivity of the faith—to tear down the walls that humankind had built up around God's true nature. He did not do this by changing the law or by diplomatically negotiating principles between nations. His mission was never political but spiritual. However, the heartbeat of a nation always changes as its heart changes. After the death and resurrection of Christ, the faith was still exclusive, not based on earthly nationality, but on heavenly citizenship. It was based on a person's heart and a new disposition toward God that was given and not attained through works. Christ united all nations no longer by geographical or cultural boundaries but by the boundaries of the human heart and mind. Christ made public the true faith that was once only available to the religious and cultural elite, and indeed was never available in its fullness. This provided everyone with an equal opportunity, no matter their origin, to engage in a relationship with the living God and to be set free from their sins. Although the faith changed from making open access to the Father available only to the Hebrews, the faith was still exclusive, but the aspect of that exclusivity was altered. Now salvation is no longer dependent on nationality or on the practice of certain traditions, but solely on belonging to Christ and following the authority of His commands by the power of the Holy Spirit that came from the Father.

The early church struggled to understand the paradigm shift of the faith but was extremely grateful that salvation had been made available to all, namely the gentiles. They realized that originally as outsiders, many were participants in and recipients of a life that would never have been available if it had not been for Christ. Every aspect of their life was urged to be lived in constant rejoicing and faithfulness, even though many of them were mocked, beaten, starved, imprisoned, tortured, and martyred. The fact that these heroes held fast to the teachings of the Christ and His apostles throughout the fiercest era of persecution for doing so indicates the genuine faith of the early church, and demolishes the popular theory that the early Christians were only generating a myth. They simply did not stand to gain anything of worldly advancement by following the *true* path of the Christian.

The apostles of Christ are some of the clearest proofs of the truth that is in the Way. After Christ's ascension, they hid until the arrival of the Holy Spirit. After this, they were no longer hiding, but boldly proclaiming the truth of the gospel throughout the nations, regardless of the fatal consequences most of them would face as a result, as many of them were persecuted to the point of death for their beliefs. Their followers were then subjected to such evils as imprisonment, torture, being burned alive, beheaded, and forced to fight wild animals in Roman arenas. Each of them, being much closer to the events than we are geographically, culturally and temporally, was convinced to the point of forsaking their earthly lives and following the teachings of Christ, even if it led them to a violent end like the founder of the faith.

Today in America, Christians face a different type of challenge. Christians likely do not face the same levels of hardships their predecessors faced. However, as Jesus said, when we decide to follow Him, if we give it our all, our reality will be altered in some way. We may lose our jobs for sharing Jesus with a coworker, or we may alienate friends and family because of what it truly means to believe. We do not generally face death or imprisonment today, although many other heroes do in other parts of the world. However, the dichotomy of Christianity and everything else remains, even in

America, often causing dismay and offense to those on the outside. This is a "problem" that will never be solved unless the original precepts of Christianity are abandoned, or the entire world is genuinely converted. Even in the earliest age of Christianity, there were teachers and prophets who desired to acclimate the force of the Gospel of Christ to the modern worldviews.

Today, those attitudes remain. However, the purest form of Christianity is the form that does not abandon itself for the sake of worldly gain or reputation. (I'll have to admit my shortcoming in this area.) This is the form that is at once the most foreign and offensive to outsiders, as well as the most genuine and respected. The early Christians showed either what it meant to stay true to the principles of Christ or to conform to the pattern of the world, and every Christian since then has shown to the world the same polarization within the church. One stays true to the character of Christ and promotes Him, while another casts doubt upon everything about Christ.

GOOD VERSUS EVIL

Of things that exist, some exist by
nature, some from other causes.

—Aristotle

"THE MOUNTAINS ARE MY CHURCH." As a snowboarder and an avid hiker, this was often my philosophy before coming to Christ, and admittedly at times afterward. This is still the philosophy of many of my friends who love the mountains. I think the point of slogans like this is to say that everyone has a version of church for themselves, no matter where they go to find it; one may find it in an actual church, another in a Buddhist temple, another by snowboarding, and another at a bar. The way society views "church" as a relative thing illustrates a moral ultimatum. Either there is a hierarchy of moral ideals on this planet or each person's version of morality is created equal, with rights that cannot be revoked, like a declaration of independence for our ideals. If the latter is the case, then I have no *right* to think *my* version of church in any way better than or superior to another person's, who considers my church no more or less *right* than his frequenting a bar. The world's version of church in particular differentiates between the way Christians and outsiders view morality in general. One person may believe in loving one's neighbor even when it comes at a cost. Another may believe in hurting one's neighbor for one's own benefit. Neither of them can objectively be more or less good or evil if morality is only relative, which is a logical outworking of the survival of the fittest paradigm. Obviously, the concept of the latter being seen as a better person is ridiculous, but the principle of moral relativity is the result of a mandatory equality of worldviews, which many believe is the correct form of morality simply because it is seen to be more tolerant or fair.

The fallacy of moral relativity largely ignores the truth about human nature, even if the highest view of morality is the most popular at the time, or what is authorized by national law—a few examples being Nazi Germany or Soviet Russia, in which differing levels of moral and human values were appropriated by the state, which believed itself to be the highest power. Humanity always operates with some notion of objective moral absolutes, otherwise people like the leaders of the nations mentioned will never struggle to implement and defend their own notions of things like justice and righteousness. If the reader thinks what I just wrote is absolutely wrong, they just proved me right by indicating a defense of what they believe to be an absolute standard of truth, a superior standard to mine by which the reader operates. This perceived higher standard of truth cannot exist by the nature of the total moral relativity that atheism predicates. Likewise, most atheists are not going around advocating lying, stealing, and killing because they know such things are wrong. But if there is no objective moral standard outside of one's own interpretation or society's collective and codified standards of right and wrong, then we are all following laws that are in no way true, laws that are always prone to shift with the times even if they seem momentarily true and fixed to us.

Moral relativity has been a practical device for hiding all kinds of evil from differing societies and generations—an example being soviet citizens turning over family members to be tortured and killed in prison camps for the most mundane types of transgressions against the beloved party, the entity substituted for God which well-conditioned citizens revered as the ultimate standard of truth and righteousness.

Such instances of moral relativity are often the result of a completely secularized culture and worldview. If they are followed to their ends, the societies in which they're followed would crumble into the simultaneous chaos and tyranny of everybody following their own equal views of what is right, while trying to assert those views upon and over others, often through coercion and cruelty. Such a society's beginnings may look like a culture totally sold out to postmodernity—a philosophy in which every truth can be deconstructed or enshrined based on a whim. For one person in such a society, it is right to kill; for another, it is not right. No one can argue objectively which person is actually right, because both ideals are by nature created equal, and both truths can be simultaneously deconstructed. From a distance, the idea of equality of ideas seems utopian enough, and the rejection of that equality via the upholding of certain standards of truth feels like discrimination. After all, if humankind is created equal, shouldn't its ideas (philosophies, religions, etc.) all be considered equal as well? Under the microscopes of moral relativity and postmodernity, Christian absolutism seems absurdly harsh, legalistic, abrasive, and constraining. It infringes on the modern paradigm of privatization and pluralization, as well as the modern interpretation of rights. In other words, "do as you will" becomes the highest law, and anyone who questions it becomes a transgressor.

New and modernized morality is always challenging and undermining the ethical and legal "norms" of society. When the way things ought to be gets in the way of the way we want things to be, we often reform the way things ought to be into the way we want things to be. When this process happens as a result of faulty reasoning and personal or group ambitions, things often simply become what they ought not to be for everyone, and ultimately what no one wants. This manipulative vision, which often begins with a reevaluation of certain givens, usually results in a deformity of the most obvious standards in humanity, and thus deforms humanity itself in some way, shape or form. This line of reasoning is the mathematical outcome of a purely Darwinian social psychology as it pertains to morality, for atheistic naturalism must do away with metaphysical things like the soul in order to remain consistent, and it is only arbitrary any time a concept like the "soul" is invoked under such a psychology. In atheistic naturalism, every person's morality, as well as cultural morality, is simply the result of a purely evolutionary process in both the psychological and ethical development of the individual mind, and the sociological development of a cultural or societal attitude as a whole. If this is the case, then each person's morality is either genuine enough to be taken seriously and adhered to or foolish enough to be ridiculed and ignored. All standards must be universally recognized, and so none are until they prove to be of personal or societal benefit, a benefit which all too often is fleeting and comes at a high cost to others. All ideals boil right back down to their base of total subjectivity as humankind invents, revises, and upholds nothing more than its own personal law.

The attack on Christian morality can be at once an attack on its authority, its simplicity, and its exclusivity. The morality demanded by the God of the Bible would have to be a universal morality, meaning that it holds true for every individual and it matters outside of what the individual thinks of it. It doesn't matter whether or not you agree with the law of gravity. If you jump off of a skyscraper, the ground rules still apply. The law in the Bible is so concise that it fit onto two stone tablets and still maintains "relative" order over humanity, although it remains under constant public scrutiny. People may find it hard to believe that the full extent of positive human moral behavior could fit concisely into Ten Commandments, and still harder to believe that half of those commandments are inextricably linked to how we treat God. Though people may find the Ten Commandments hard to believe, they actually prove them even harder to follow. It is only when these Commandments are broken that we see the true manifestation of human brokenness permeate individuals and society. Jesus even summarized these Ten Commandments as such: love God with everything you are and love your neighbor as yourself. The inversions of such a precise law usually result in nothing good.

The world criticizes Christianity for being at once too harsh and too simplistic. Many want rules that are easier to follow and make them look smarter. Atheists can be quick to point out the "harshness" and "simplicity" of God's law, especially in the pages of the Old Testament—even if they aren't always willing to admit what has historically come as a result of implementing laws from an atheistic worldview, laws that are as complex and hard to interpret as they are vague and haphazard. But complex laws and philosophies are not always just or wise laws and philosophies.

For many atheists, *if the God of the Bible exists,* He must be a ruthless dictator, incapable of moral compassion or sensible judgement. Critics point to certain Old Testament behavior of God in His wrath and judgement to fortify their presuppositions, believing His perspective to be as narrow as those who follow His path. In such a caricature, God is regarded as an unenlightened simpleton or an evil king, and His outdated laws are likewise relics of the Dark Ages. The new age revivalist who sees the universe as falling within the relativistic "order" of natural enlightenment doesn't take Jesus's two commandments very seriously, because they deal precisely with what transcends the natural—love. If anything, these laws are just another bumper sticker slogan to be read alongside the others. Their stunning simplicity and universality don't merit much room for interpretation.

Intellectuals would rather have thousands of pages of secular psychology and sociology to prove what has already been stated clearly in the Bible—the fundamental flaw in the human condition is sin. Their hope for righteousness transfers from God—who is the source of that righteousness—to a new humankind where a perfect empire may finally emerge. Humankind may finally become aware of its more prehistoric and unevolved mannerisms, and thus evolve past them. By understanding the *true* nature of evil and thrusting aside the outdated doctrine of sin, we can at last revolt against the uneducated and the unevolved. But apparently, as we've seen in the last century, this more evolved law of human harmony can only be written after all of its attempts are systematically tried and failed, with the trials and failures happening under the same material banner. Only then will we finally arrive at our utopian destination after all levels of misery have been achieved. How can one still recite the old law in the presence of this totalitarian *newness*? For though the new is built from the old, the old is rejected because it disgusts a fallen world. God's morality and wisdom, along with the unfit, must be purged from society if the fittest are to survive.

We cannot escape the persistence of the Ten Commandments within the laws of all human societies throughout all their histories. Common sense laws which forbid murder and stealing have always strengthened the societies which employed them, and societies that permitted such things, even temporarily, have been judged harshly by history. Likewise, when human tendencies such as covetousness and adultery occur, or are allowed to be organized within society at large (the desecration of private property in communism being an example of the former), it is usually a sign of those individuals' or societies' moral degradation. An inescapable fact remains behind those laws, whether they exist to guard from inward or outward transgressions. God created the laws for humanity just as He created the laws of nature such as gravity and oxygen that keep us alive. We cannot escape either the physical or spiritual standards that reside within the varying conditions of our outward surroundings and our inward souls. As creator, God had the divine right to create any laws He wanted. The laws which He created are today scoffed at as too harsh or too simplistic, yet no man or woman has been able to follow them to the letter, with one exception.

People often wonder why their personal lives and the world around them seems to be imploding, or at least decaying. People disagree with the law of God because it contradicts the law set forth by the flesh, which is set in place to enshrine the desire to be our own gods. God's law is not too elementary or too harsh for humans. If it was, it never would have been established *for our benefit.* Humans think that we are much happier following our own, more self-inclusive laws, but we prove only the clashing chaos and contradiction that dwell within the fallible and mortal fabric of those laws. Suddenly God's fixed and ancient law becomes more complex, universal, and loving than any revolutionary and shifting set of human laws we may imagine. This phenomenon is further proven by the characteristic human tendency to mimic elements of God's original law, such as truthfulness and punishment for crimes, in order to justify our own parallel standards of things like honesty and justice. This simply shows another system that God designed to be as inseparable as our nervous system, namely the conscience.

The divine law is seen through a secular lens as something that will imprison humankind behind the bars of old religion. However, by fleeing the boundaries that God set in place for us, we have found our way into a new prison which grants only the illusion of freedom. We acclimate well to this prison because it makes so much sense to us. It is familiar, consisting of our own handiwork. Its architecture and furnishing appear beautiful to us. And it is what we know. Like Plato's cave, to emerge from the shadows that make up our imitated reality is a fearful thought. The resulting culture of our world has all our favorite pastimes and passions—all our pleasures and guilty secrets. We find our livelihoods in this prison of our own architecture. But the prison often lacks in its essence the full presence of things like truth and justice which were inherent in God's immutable construct for the endurance of humankind. What we get from human invention is undeniably much more like a shadow of things like truth and justice.

In our prison, we have pretended that all men and women are equal, but in reality, we are superior to others. This is why every person at one point or another rejects the moral law and the moral law giver. We believe them to be beneath us. The higher law undermines our own sense of superiority. Yet people demonstrate in their conscience a desire to escape the prison of shadows, which has resulted in an increasingly obscure and relativistic moral law, which often times desecrates the most basic tenets of humanity. As time goes by, the faulty foundation of our own law becomes another house of cards.

We cannot deny that within each of us, there is both a tendency to basically understand right and wrong as well as a tendency to challenge and transgress those standards. The fact that basic moral instincts, like to refrain from killing fifty people or to take a bite out of another man's sandwich, are internally hardwired into us is an indication of some sort of absolute moral standard that exists objectively. If this standard exists objectively and universally (which is the only way to explain the continuing function of the conscience, however vulnerable it may be to being seared), and even apart from societal standards, then it no longer can be explained away as an evolutionary by-product or a product of social experiments. Its universality and absolutism together indicate its transcendence. Again, if humans automatically gain a larger perspective of an advancing morality in the natural processes of evolution, how do we explain the horrors of the latest century, or our tendency to objectively judge such horrors as horrors at all today? If the most evolved form of human reasoning led to a morally superior existence, then we ought to have advanced past such common sins, as well as their resulting shame and judgement. But if our evolving natural reasoning tells us again tomorrow that it would be better for the survival of our race to eliminate other races, along with the sick, the disabled, the weak, *or the unborn,* then why shouldn't we? What transcendent standard can visibly stop us?

Morality cannot be looked at solely from a naturalistic perspective, because it cannot be seen at all, any more than gravity can be seen. It is the invisible agent that keeps us from falling into chaos, and it is not of our own design any more than our nervous systems are. It must be examined for what it is—universal, absolute, and therefore transcendent. It is just as wrong to kill in Utah as it would be to kill in Timbuctoo, even though the human law and punishment may differ for such a crime in each place. Objective moral standards are not solely geographically applicable. They are not solely suited to one's individual preference. Nor are they solely applicable based on popular consensus. The objective existence of any single moral standard at all therefore is an obvious dilemma for the evolutionary interpretation of good and evil.

Though our conscience often feels subjective and varies from person to person based on things like temperament or sensibility, every human being has one—just as every human being has a unique fingerprint. The innate knowledge of right and wrong shows that the ideas of right and wrong exist outside both the self and the community at large. This makes no sense in a purely naturalistic framework. Anywhere one may find intelligence or information such as the innate intelligibility of basic laws of morality, there must be mind that communicated that intelligence. In the same way, there is an inversion of this principle. Evil exists and escapes intelligibility, thus indicating what is opposite to itself, even to the dullest person. Evil comes from the erasure, the desecration, the deconstruction, the contradiction, and the ignorance of the objectivity of morality, and thus inherent human value. Ignorance of this ignorance doesn't negate this law of evil. In the spiritual sense, evil comes much more simply from turning away from God. These two precepts corroborate the first four Commandments as they pertain to God and the last six as they pertain to others. The latter is visible in history and the former requires faith. Both are contingent on one another and so neither can be done away with.

An objective and universal moral law logically indicates a moral law giver, just as a man standing behind bars logically indicates the presence of a criminal justice system. One either must ascribe the mind behind such an objective and universal moral law to the mind of the "greater good" and the consensus of morality which comes from society at large or on God's original law. Either morality is based on the psychological and sociologically evolving whims of the people or it is based on Christ's immutable words. It either grows naturally from those who have defined and redefined moral expectations throughout the ages and generations or is fixed forever in the expectations and the revelation of a transcendent *one who knows*. Usually the best option for societies is a combination of both. One who bases morality on pure subjectivity either of the individual or the populous is doomed to ultimately disregard objective human value on one level or another. Whereas one who bases morality solely on notions of the supernatural and rejects the laws of their nation as such is bound to coerce others or to follow a notion of law which is largely based on their interpretation of the law as it is—which will exclude the complex and interpersonal elements of just laws enacted by sovereign governments for the mutual benefit of society (a system which the Bible itself commands us to live under). God blends these ideas in the manifestation of His Word, who came in adherence to both the law of God and the rule of the governing power of His time, even though the latter was inferior to the former, secularized, and often oppressive.

Which view of morality agrees with the evidence brought forth in the pages of human history and in the complex choices we make every day? Which view of morality appeals most to the logic of the soul, or even merits the existence of a soul? For the naturalist, the subjective view makes the most sense. They believe that it is no intellectual copout to pontificate upon the *true* origin of morality. The origin of morality, like the origin of species, can be scientifically traced alongside the evolution of humanity. Rationality and intelligence, in this view, led to our superiority in every sense of the word, including morality—only the fittest survived. Evolution led us to learn how to better advance our species and get along with one another. If only that were true. More often than not, the material pursuit of ethical knowledge for the sake of avoiding morality's theological implications has ended altogether in failure and madness. One has only to study history for five minutes to know that this view is flawed and fatal. When we seat the origin and persistence of morality solely among the given population, and no higher, we will always emerge with a relativity, a blend of good and evil. Whether it is evil disguised as good, good disguised as evil, good mistaken for evil, evil mistaken for good, or a little of both remains to be seen. This relativity is the result of human consensus. Ultimately, it is not a matter of which one emerges triumphant in a democratic system, but which is more adequately highlighted by people. But even the most passionate or persuasive are prone to the often unconscious human condition of valuing self above both God and others even as they advocate or legislate. If there is no standard of judgement over the higher consensus, the result will be arbitrary.

In the naturalistic definition of morality, it becomes impossible to argue any sensible basis for one's own morality without identifying the foundation thereof as either one's own opinion or the opinion of the higher consensus. There is no adequate way of concretely determining which ground is higher, for often the individual can be more right even when his or her opinion is more unpopular. Moral evolution offers no definitive low or highpoint to the moral hierarchy. It is because of this conundrum that no better conclusion has yet emerged than the existence of a transcendent moral law. This conclusion, the walls of which are unlikely to be breached, indicates a transcendent and authoritative moral law maker as well as moral law breakers who have always remained underneath and often in opposition to that transcendence and authority. This reality is best captured in scripture.

How do we adequately place the identity of the constitutive and transcendent being who implemented the law? Which law are we at once most familiar with and most tempted to transgress? Again, it's the Ten Commandments, written by the finger of God Himself. We all have innate knowledge of God in our inmost being, though we often don't admit it. Yet we all at one point or another deny God in order to follow our own desires. As we become increasingly deaf and blind to Him, the relevance or likeliness of His authority in our lives retreats into doubt. This occurs through a process of self-justification of the individual for the wrong they do, as they promote themselves among others and assert themselves over others. We are all tempted to fashion replacements for ourselves to fill the God-shaped hole—which is another phrase to describe the meaninglessness that is inherent in godlessness, in this case as it pertains to interpreting goodness.

We have all probably at one time or another used God's name as a curse word. I stole many candy bars in my youth. We've all lied, likely. Most people who have a beating heart have looked at another person lustfully. Indeed, nobody's perfect. God's law, mimicked in our conscience, shows that "The heart is deceitful above all things and beyond cure. Who can understand it?" (Jeremiah 17:9). When confronted with the original moral law given in the Bible, an honest person cannot help but admit its eternal relevance, as well as admit their failure to adhere to it. The problem is clearly laid out, as well as the solution.

IN IT TOGETHER

Like the blind we grope along the wall,
feeling our way like men without eyes. At
midday we stumble as if it were twilight;
among the strong, we are like the dead.

—Isaiah 59:10

CHRIST PROVED WHO HE IS by saving me from what I was. If people were honest with themselves, I think they'd likely turn back the clock to change a mistake or two they made in their past. Sometimes we may wish that we could project our wiser selves back through time to visit the younger, more foolish versions of ourselves in order to talk some sense into them. Many are haunted by the sins of their past. This haunting is not always from damage done to us by other people but the damage we are able to do. Scripture tells us that this is because of our separation from God. As we discussed in the previous chapter, every person adheres and appeals to a certain standard of morality, whether it be subjective or objective. This is why we generally don't run around killing people. The last chapter also touched on the failure of a naturalistic explanation to provide a realistic framework to explain why this is, or to explain the human conscience. This is why societies built purely on subjective morality and atheistic, evolutionary materialism so often resulted in nihilism and atrocity. Good behavior in the natural sense is only a result of the evolution of a moral code within the development of societal and individual life experiences, or certain cultural visions. Therefore, the standards are always subject to amendment. In such a world, there can be no transcendence or standard of perfection above the state, just as there can be no higher standard of truth than the information provided by the state. With this summary in mind, the following section will discuss the deeper reality of the discussion on morality, and the overwhelming likeliness of the Christian explanation for why humans naturally tend to fall short.

The doctrine of sin still best describes the never-ending human moral "evolution" and argument of moral definition among the continuing phenomenon of individual and societal moral degeneration. The doctrine of sin is simply *simple*, too simple for the wisdom of the world. Its simplicity shrouds it with the doubts of the enlightened while safeguarding its form throughout the rise and fall of countless generations and kingdoms. Sin originated in the doubt and twisting of God's words and persists largely by convincing the individual that it is not present, and confusing us as to its mechanisms—the definition of evil simply could not be defined within the limited terms of human knowledge, as it still escapes our comprehension whenever it is present. The one falling word of sin is a contradiction of the standing Word of God—*logos*—which is the seat of all divine logic and reason. This is why sin is at once so reasonable to the world and unreasonable to God. Sin is not only a transgression of morality, but of reality as God intended it. Satan is able to tempt us anew by presenting his lies as the new, more advanced word. But as a plagiarist, he is only able to take what already is and contradict it. To claim to have the new, more advanced word is a great and fatal boast, but many under the guise of the serpent still cling to it today. The serpent's promise of freedom through prideful and worldly logic subjects the transgressors of God's Word to a prison of death through knowledge. His promise of what could be was only an inversion of what actually was. After all, sin was just one little bite, it was so simple for humanity to enter into such a revolutionary and complex kind of knowledge—it would take only one bite to explain what truly gave rise to the world. The transgression did give rise to a new world, but it was a world of evil and suffering. At once, the transgression tells a child to lie to and dishonor his parents and a dictator to oppress an entire race. Its origin sounds to many like a myth about a talking snake. It has no appeal to the reach of human intellect, for it is human intellect that it beguiles. It does not seem as comprehensive and conclusive as the volumes of secular explanations for why things are the way they are.

The wisdom of the world is always bent on explicating evil along with everything else that emerged throughout the unguided moral processes of the world. The truth, however, is much simpler in cause and grander in scale. Biting into the fruit contained a promise of pleasure, so to speak. But the result of the action greatly outweighed the temporary taste and fleeting knowledge it may have had. The doctrine of sin still is the best and only explanation for evil's continued existence as the thorn in humanity's side simply because it acknowledges evil's continued existence and does not explain it away. Sin, not psychological, emotional, or behavioral issues, explains the iniquity of every individual, giving insight to the true nature of selfish, foolish, and wicked human behavior. Sin is the beginning, the definition, and the diagnosis of evil present in individuals and the communities they constitute. Its reality and perpetual condition is increasingly denied in the name of certain sciences, for the existence of sin is spiritual and not physical. Sinfulness will always be impossible to scientifically prove for a person of high intellect and obvious to any child who has even the dullest sense of justice. The uninterrupted spiritual aspect of sin is likewise why no human thus far has been capable of escaping its grasp, except one. The attempt of secularism to blind us to sin's reality is no antidote for the negative side of the human condition.

It appears that there is no limit to a person's ability to degenerate and self-destruct, even when they often take every available measure to avoid doing so. To deny any personal recognition of our sin is simply to evade genuine self-knowledge. This denial shows that we are influenced by a deep deception, one that arises from within our flesh to hide from us the pain that is within us: "Each heart knows its own bitterness" (Proverbs 14:10); "The heart is deceitful above all things, and desperately wicked" (Jeremiah 17:8). The heart can easily be ensnared by such things as hopelessness, darkness, and doubt. These are a result of the denial of God's Word: "The mind of sinful man is death" (Romans 8:6); "Did God really say 'you shall not eat from any tree in the garden'?" (Genesis 3:1). Sin manipulates truth. It confuses, allures, and ultimately destroys. The more one gets used to this manipulation and denuding of truth and what's right, the more one conforms to a warped version of the path God intended for us. The condition of sin causes us to walk through life with an increasingly distorted spiritual vision as the lie disguises itself as the truth and the truth as the lie. This distortion can be reinforced by many things, both seen and unseen. Just like a disease, the condition progresses as long as it is left untreated. It grows within the prison bars of doubt and resentment where it began. Eventually, our sin and selfish desire to be our own god will eradicate any notion of the Word. Spiritual deafness and blindness become trademarks of the human condition. It is likewise hard to see the full impact of our sin on the world around us, and we cannot escape it on our own.

One who is under the impression that sin *is* natural to humanity and for their own benefit, is actually acting in a way which was meant to be contrary to the nature of humanity. The trouble is that we are all under this impression at one point or another, so we all act in ways that contradict what God made us for. Such an impression and the actions that result from it have been consistent within the world pattern since the beginning, reaffirming our faulty perception of naturalness in the unnatural human condition: "All a man's ways seem right to him, but the Lord weighs the heart" (Proverbs 21:2); "If then the light within you is darkness, how great is that darkness!" (Matthew 6:23); "What has been will be again, what has been done will be done again; there is nothing new under the sun" (Ecclesiastes

1:9). One may say that the only thing that has been universally known to all is what was never meant to be known at all. This helps explain the ongoing presence of evil *alongside* the existence of a good and all powerful God.

A child's disobedience can happen in a few ways—by questioning the truth of the parents' words, by manipulating the parents' rules for the child's benefit, or by rejecting the parents' words and rules altogether. In the third chapter of Genesis, sin operates in all three of these ways. In the garden of Eden, the serpent challenges Eve to know her potential divinity. Ironically, she is told that her divinity can only be revealed by means of transgressing God's divine law. This step may have seemed counterintuitive, but it was not only faulty logic that convinced her that the serpent was correct. It was the hope of personal passions coming to fruition and the promise of an unknown pleasure that transcended what could be found in the garden. "When the woman saw that the fruit of the tree was good for food and pleasing to the eye, and desirable for gaining wisdom, she took some and ate it" (Genesis 3:6). When passion is included in a lie that has an element of the truth, it is a recipe for disaster. To most, the initial transgression seems like an obvious mistake. But one must remember that it is through interpretation of God's law that we assume transgression of the law is beneficial to ourselves and even an improvement upon the law. It is our passion that blinds us to the absurdity of this.

Sin is a deceptive illusion. It disguises itself as being godlike and transcendent, even though it is Godless and causes us to stoop down to where we are not meant to be. Its perceived benefit appears fruitful at first, but in the end, it results in deep internal and external consequences. The serpent knew the enticement of rebellion. But he also knew that it led to punishment. To convince Eve, he revealed the first premise of the child's three transgressions—denying the authority of God's Word. The other two premises unfold in a split second, leading to a rebellion due to a blindness to the consequence of transgression. Humankind still sins with the same intent. When we consider culture's increasing hostility toward God in the secular age, the doctrine of original sin becomes much more realistic.

The biblical doctrine of sin is still undeniably relevant, especially as culture at large insinuates and propagates its undeniable irrelevance. It is exact in describing the depravity of the human condition and is one of the most convincing keys to unlocking the truth of Christianity. There is simply no better spiritual diagnosis of our spiritual disease available. A fall is always coming when we try to climb what we cannot climb, even if we momentarily recognize the possibility of a fall and continue to climb anyway. In the wake of the recognition of peril, fear troubles the one who halfheartedly believes a fall is coming, but this fear is often not enough to curb ambition. It is really only self-justification and ascendency apart from the work of God that one is seeking. Self-absolvent and false repentance of sin is an even more glaring rejection and on a mass scale they perpetuate the world pattern. But, to our displeasure, the truth will always indicate our corruption if it is to cure us of it, just as a doctor must provide a diagnoses before he prescribes a treatment.

The reality of sin in general and personal sin in particular is difficult to perceive apart from a revelation from God as to the extent of one's own opposition to God. Sin doesn't make sense apart from the existence of God. And why should it? God's existence predicates His standards, and thus our falling short of them. This is why Jesus tells of the Holy Spirit's conviction of sin. A person's spiritual condition in relation to God must be made known to them, and often our pride, or denial of God's existence and thus His standards, impact our ability to interpret human behavior through this lens of original sin. Sin doesn't make sense to the world pattern. It is too simplistic, too mythological, and too reductionist. Therefore, apart from the divine revelation of personal sin, many human revelations have taken its place. For example, many come to the conclusion, convenient as it may be, that the doctrine of sin is only a primitive description of the more negative aspects of our residual animal nature and our survival of the fittest psyche. This explanation is suited to make sense from a biological standpoint, but it also conveniently absolves the self from accountability to any objective moral standards so that one may remain in their patterns of behavior while claiming those patterns to be natural, as unnatural as they may become.

Naturalistic morality implies that to kill, lie, steal, and destroy is indefinitely embedded in the evolutionary ancestry of the human organism, yet they do not currently fit our more evolved human ideals. By such reasoning, evil, as it were, will occasionally resurface, but evolution, over time, will decrease its power—whether or not events in recent human history have stood in stark contrast to this concept. To explain sin and evil away naturalistically like this has proven historically to be a way to trivialize, rationalize, and justify many kinds of evil. As a result, the definition and presence of evil becomes more and more meaningless as sin is allowed to grow throughout our lifetimes, and indeed throughout generations, under the myth of it being the natural state of humanity. Quite simply, when its definition comes under threat, human perception of its presence often comes under threat as well. Sin and evil are inescapable in both the evolutionary and spiritual perspectives. But in the former, wickedness is only another result of brain chemistry and social interactions somehow going awry, nothing more, nothing deeper or more primary. The spiritual component of good and evil must be denied by logic of a purely evolutionary perspective, hence the description of and adherence to certain standards of morality must be reduced to nothing more than a phenomenon or series thereof which can be either held fast or discarded based on people's arbitrary will. Whether humanity clashes or embraces ultimately means nothing on a biological or cosmic level. We emerge, we struggle, and we die—there is no objective right or wrong in any of it—whether or not those who do not believe God recognize that, to whatever varying degree, this challenge continues to be the inevitable outcome of the methodologically naturalistic view on sin and evil.

The good news is that this view is reductionist, and it is designed to trick us into believing that it's true. One goal of sin is to blend good and evil in order to fit them into the confines of the human mind, confusing them and perhaps turning them into abstract ideas that we can take or leave as we please—as well as ultimately promoting ourselves, in our false system of weights and measures, to the status of definitive judges between the two. We justify evil actions by blending them with our newer and more advanced notion of good and evil in the name of knowledge, of course this notion also goes hand in hand with self-justification. This knowledge, which was never intended, lives on in our flesh, is encouraged by the devil, and is reproduced endlessly within the world pattern. Therefore, we end up forgetting, misinterpreting, or willfully ignoring which is which. The result looks an awful lot like lots of people hurting lots of other people in a vast array of ways over a long period of time. Such a view can appear very pessimistic, as it denies people in general the right to claim an inherent temperament of goodness, and reinforces an inherent temperament of any given human heart as being deceitful, above all other things. This is also why horrible things can be done by the "optimist" and wonderful things by the "pessimist." Adolf Hitler considered himself an evolutionary agent of sorts acting to bring about the next step of the natural selection of the human race, and his party likewise considered the weak and disabled members of society as a disposable hindrance to humanity. He was evolutionarily optimistic that humanity would one day be less hindered by what he considered to be its most crippled parts. More disturbing still, he convinced a large part of Germany of the reasonableness and necessity of Nazi motives by appealing to the somewhat newfound materialistic ideals of the survival of the fittest. The driving force of the evolution theory in this and other ideologies is largely ignored or denied altogether. However, if this perspective is true, then how can we argue anything resembling good and evil, without only invoking things like our own common sense as the determining factor? All ideas, good or bad, would boil down to subjectivity and lose their meaning, no matter how obvious they may seem to the majority of people, many of which likewise adhere to more naturalistic explanations. Yet we see atheists and believers alike operating under their convictions, convictions that *by nature* should not be there if we are just random piles of atoms without any objective, absolute, and therefore transcendent guiding principles. Even in the increasing cultural demand for total subjectivity and an eventual breach into the next stage of our moral evolution, there is no possible abandonment of the knowledge of good and evil. The existence of an atheist's conscience is indeed a sizeable roadblock for atheism.

The account in Genesis clearly frames the distinction between good and evil by placing this distinction outside humanity itself, insisting upon the *fact* that sin is in part a result of a conscious and perpetual transgression against the divine law which transcends human authorship. It is in part an active agent of darkness and chaos that resides within the human heart. This doctrine is simple, yet its simplicity does not make it reductionist, but observable and undeniable. The truth does not reduce the obvious choices in what we do solely to colliding factors of chance and chaos. In fact, often it is the sinner's goal to obtain total control over the chaos in their lives which they do not yet recognize as sin that leads them to prolong the chaotic results of that sin. Every person is confronted by a series of choices. These choices are always a result of our relation to God, others, and ourselves. Usually these choices are aimed, like an arrow, at the target of restoring peace in these three relations. The unnatural human inclination frustrates our honest aim by placing these relations out of balance; shooting the arrow becomes like hitting a moving target that's in two places at once. For we are trying to act upon a law we really do not believe is there, to love God and others without insight as to why.

Jesus taught that true peace occurs when we put God first, our neighbor second, while dismissing ourselves. One may assume the self to be third, although I do not believe it is explicitly mentioned in the equation. In fact, humans are taught to be sel*fless* in the Word.

This is actually what humanity is seeking, the weightlessness of selflessness taught and exemplified through Christ; "For my yoke is easy and my burden is light" (Matthew 11:30). But every person fails. By placing self above God and others, we unknowingly bog ourselves down in sin and the fear of man; it is by this process that our understanding is darkened. In our search for freedom from the prison of the self, we look solely to the self for the escape plan. We know that our relationships are broken, and we keep asking *ourselves* why—as well as trying to fix them in our own strength.

The loving summation of the law put forth by Jesus fell into the categories of God and others. Any activity focused purely on the ambition of the self is therefore sinful, and much of our ambitions, if examined honestly, have an element of promoting our own virtuosity or status. Just as sin is destructive, deconstructive, and rebellious at its core, it is also rooted in *selfishness*. This, before all other elements of doubt, is what humankind simply cannot surpass on its own; to outdo the self by the power of the self would be redundant. For example, Adam and Eve's temptation was so convincing because of the invitation to stop worrying about what God said and turn their thoughts inward, to *their own true* divinity in order to understand and use their "full" potential. By obeying the void law of transcendence through rebellion they unlocked sin's full potential. Adam and Eve's actions were not for the good of anyone else but arose because of the promise of an increase in personal knowledge, power, and status—that of a god. To become gods, they chose the path that led away from God.

Sin is extremely deceptive and alluring because it uses our passions and desires against us. More often than not, it can camouflage as what is right and good and true for us, often posing as something natural to us, as stated, while implying that alternative virtues such as forgiveness and chastity are the truly unnatural things. Much evil can be done in the name of what is perceived as good or beneficial when the standards of what's good and beneficial are subjective relative to our passions and desires, or even inverted to adhere to our passions and desires. Our own end becomes our only means, corrupting our vision. Self-purposing virtuosity and our perceived divinity become the lens by which we see everything and the scale by which we weigh all that comes into our hands. Apart from God, we are only capable of reproducing religions of the self, by the self and for the self.

Everything that grows begins first as a small seed. From the seed of self-righteousness, true evil so often visibly manifests. "How can you say to your brother, 'let me take the speck out of your eye,' when all the time there is a plank in your own eye?" (Matthew 7:4). Unfortunately, this is how humans view one another still, Christ's perspective on self-righteousness is as true as ever today. When we perceive ourselves as better than others, we hijack the truth and distort the goodness of God. His meanings are only to be interpreted for our own ends. Thus we invent a faulty structure of morality or religion built on some caricatured foundation borrowed from the truth within the Judeo-Christian principles. The structure we create is simply much more appealing to us because it was made by us. To the world, it often appears as though we are making all the right choices and moving in the right direction when we follow our own law, but this is only because we are choosing the very same misdirection of the world's strategy. The simultaneous rejection and plagiarism of the Word constitutes the mind-set of humanity. The Word, in its truth and immutability, is strange and perverse in the eyes of the world system, especially the more one deviates from the misdirection of that system. "Enter through the narrow gate. For wide is the gate and broad is the path that leads to destruction" (Matthew 7:13).

Sin is the knowledge of good and evil, where they have come to shake hands and get to know one another, to make a polite compromise. They become friends and trade ideas, even identities. Godliness is wrested and inverted to fit the ideas and identities of the new "forward-thinking" person. The picture of what is truly right becomes grossly outdated and obsolete, lost in the accounts of history. Just as in every preceding section, the further we get from God in our interpretation of things, the closer we come to individual and societal foolishness: "The fear of the Lord is the beginning of Wisdom, and knowledge of the Holy One is understanding" (Proverbs 9:10). When we deny His existence, we are given a free pass to be our own judges of what constitutes good and evil. But, we are told, this power comes at a great cost to us. Jesus manifested the true and right human interpretation of the knowledge of God. He made the shifting currents of culture increasingly irrelevant. Without Him, good and evil boil down to their primordial base, and the distinction between them loses all objective rationality. They must be examined by partial interpretations. Good and evil lack ultimate essence because they cannot be seen or put into a test tube. The human heart and all of history must come to be as the new gods when we are without the one God. The new gods perpetuate the tyrannical ordering of the chaos in people's lives, who are blind to sin's reality and its dominion over humanity. Sin causes us to fall into darkness just like the very god we sought to become. Humanity has yet to outgrow this religious dogma.

The Tower of Babel is a good example of how something that seems good and constructive can actually come across as evil and destructive in God's eyes: "Then they said, 'Come, let us build ourselves a city, with a tower that reaches to the heavens, so that we may make a name for ourselves and not be scattered over the face of the whole earth.' But the Lord came down to see the city and the tower that the men were building. The Lord said, 'If as one people speaking the same language they have begun to do this, then nothing they plan to do will be impossible for them. Come, let us go down and confuse their language so they will not understand each other.' So the Lord scattered them from there over all the earth, and they stopped building the city. That is why it was called Babel—because there the Lord confused the language of the whole world. From there the Lord scattered them over the face of the whole earth" (Genesis 11:4–9). In this story, humankind reveled in their godlikeness but ultimately failed because they were operating totally in self-interest and not in the interest of God. In fact, God saw their actions as dangerous to them. In this case, unity was not strength, as this type of unity grew from a rotten root. One can't help but notice similarities between such an ancient mentality and the high-octane, big-tech, cosmological, and scientifically advanced attitude of global culture today. All of these things seem morally neutral, like building a beautiful city with a big tower in the middle of it which is incredible to behold. It seems good to be busy, driving around on our cellphones, working all day every day, always staying five minutes ahead, raking in the cash, and often being too preoccupied to give others the time of day. It seems good to have a web of interconnectivity that allows us to share virtually all of our thoughts instantaneously around the globe without being published authors—whether those thoughts are true or false, positive or negative. It seems good to have come to the brink of the theory of everything—space, time, black holes, microbes, and humans—and to no longer be plagued by the outer darkness of utter ignorance. Yet, I believe we are already seeing repercussions of this new age shadow of Babel, and if we don't keep our ambitions for ultimate utopian unity in check, ambitions which have always been alive and well within humanity, we may find ourselves much more divided and confused than we ever intended when we sought to create order from within.

LOGOS

Where is the wise man? Where is the scholar?
Where is the philosopher of this age? Has not
God made foolish the wisdom of the world?

—1 Corinthians 1:20

THE SPIRIT OF A PERSON cries out for knowledge of the right kind, to know God, and to be liberated from their bondage to sin. These questions of the spirit may be deeply related to questions of the mind. But the knowledge of the flesh and the knowledge of the world can be easily manipulated to substitute for the knowledge one truly seeks.

In the prefaced discussion, my friend and I talked about lots of spiritual and philosophical issues, to the degree that we were able. My friend was skeptical about the faith, to put it mildly, but he was very open, inquisitive, and receptive to different ideas—a trait that is all too rare these days. I remember it had been a long time since I shared my faith. One of the more interesting parts of the discussion was the apparent conundrum of free will or determinism. He could not reconcile in his mind the existence of God and the free will of humans. I felt seriously unprepared in addressing this issue, but I took a crack at it anyway, and even in our limited conversation, I found that true free will cannot be made sense of in a purely naturalistic worldview, to the contrary of much modern thinking.

How can God know the outcome of all things, and be all-powerful, and still grant us the freedom to choose? Doesn't it follow logically that He is making all our choices for us and that humankind is just a body of mindless, God-controlled automatons? These questions posed a significant challenge for me. But my simple answer was no. A good deal of this tricky speculative terrain can be navigated with a hint of common sense as we observe daily human experience, like *choosing* to get out of bed and make breakfast or *choosing* whether we make our breakfast and what we're going to eat; however, theistic determinism is to many critics of the faith a fatal flaw to the worldview we defend, even when the answer, "God grants freewill," is so simple and straightforward. Many critics think that by addressing this issue, they have backed the theist into a philosophical corner that no trinity of words can get them out of. However, the response can be quite simple and affective, and the complexity of the challenge is only used to mask its unlikeliness. To assert the impossibility of an all-powerful God existing alongside creatures whom He had granted free will is not really much of an argument at all. But for many seekers like my friend, it is actually a stumbling block to which I would pose two questions. Do you concede that it is possible that God exists? Do the daily choices you make indicate that you have free will or that you are under cosmic control?

Most will admit at least the possibility of the existence of God, of course. By this admission, they are already leaning halfway toward theism of some sort, and they may just need a slight breeze to gently push them the rest of the way. Most people will admit that they have free will every day, and if they don't admit this, they are likely not being too realistic. After all, their freewill to indicate their lack of freewill actually indicates their freewill. For how many of us are actually going about our days as victims of total mind control? I guess it may be argued that we wouldn't know it if we were. I agree that certain experiences mold us and influence our lifestyles, but to say that no one has any choice whatsoever is to blind one to reality and to conveniently absolve one of responsibility, much like the denial of sin would.

The admission of the individual that he or she demonstrates free will posits that *if* God exists as they are already admitting that He may, He must be a God who grants free will. So now they are leaning three-quarters of the way toward belief in a God who grants free will, and thus are almost swayed from materialism, which is by nature more deterministic. To be a theist with common sense, one must be free of total determinist thought. I don't know how it all works, but it just does. The next logical sequence of the conversation would be to ask honestly if free will can exist in a universe apart from God. Technically, the answer would have to be no. Let us take for example the question of why a loving God would allow so much evil in the world and follow this inquiry to its logical outworking. In asking this, one is automatically assuming there is such a thing as evil, which indicates that there also is such a thing as good. If they assume this, then they assume that there is an objective moral standard by which to judge between the two, as discussed in the previous chapters. If they assume this, then they must assume a transcendent source for this objective moral standard. Apart from God, who can be the source of this standard? Again, the use of the word "evil" in this argument undermines the natural foundation of the argument. One is forced to conclude that it makes no sense to even use the word *evil*, let alone be able to judge what constitutes its presence because, by its very substance it cannot be materialistically substantiated. It cannot definitively exist. Thus we arrive at our answer: the erasure of God from all thought only results in the total departure of any objective definition and total intellectual subjectivity, or nonsense. Therefore, we are no longer free to make *sense* of anything, or to judge or to define. Yet, as humans, we break this determinist law all the time, illustrating that we do have choice and *the knowledge of good and evil*, which is a form of bondage that itself will determine the course of our lives if ignored. Therefore, we are doomed to the sovereign decision of the cosmic conditions, and the only immediate law to be trusted is our common *senses*. Apart from this, there can be no seeable origin or foreseeable destination, and as Hume argued, we cannot even objectively trust our own senses. Therefore, in a purely materialistic worldview, humankind must be completely subject to the random forces of chaos, or to a universe with laws that do not *necessarily* need to consist, although for some reason they continue to. Even the cosmological icon Steven Hawking admitted that a purely materialistic existence would doom us to total servitude to a cruel and indifferent dominion of the universe. To the contrary of the skepticism brought about by the modern view of theistic determinism, it is really atheism that logically leads to a cruel and indifferent naturalistic determinism. Atheism ultimately contradicts what is evident and obvious in human agency.

This essay has posited that the theistic worldview does not conflict with free will and that it is impossible to philosophically exclude a higher moral standard *giver* without simultaneously undermining our own independence. How do we get from here to the God of the Bible? How do we build the bridge from human reasoning to the reasoning of God and see which God fits common sense? To the extent that this is possible through our cognitive faculties alone, I think we can come pretty close, at least closer than any other explanation.

When reading the Bible, we see from the first sentence onward a God with character and agency, who speaks words definitively, who acts, who creates. This God ascribes meaning to both the things that are and the things that we are. He clearly defines boundaries between good and evil, light and dark, life and death, sin and righteousness, and gives us the right to choose between them. The Bible, as well as human history in general, are filled with consequences and rewards for the choices, which could be seen as further evidence. Later, we see the life of the man Jesus Christ, who came to the earth *of His own free will* and yet *was sent by God*. It was *both* His own choice to lay down His life and the *will* of His Father, God. Therefore, we see in these examples and illustrations of God the correct interpretation of

God's determinism and humanity's free will, which Jesus shows are not meant to conflict, although this escapes our comprehension. The way things ought to exist is in true relationship with God's will, and that is the truer path to freedom, however painful it may be to admit.

From the beginning, humans have left this path to follow their own. It makes little sense to them that God grants a truer freedom within the parameters He has set. The garden was much smaller than the world around it, yet being banned from the garden and cast out into the world, albeit larger, was not seen as gain, but as a tremendous loss after the fall. Unless this pattern of thinking is corrected by God Himself, it results in believing God to be a sort of slave master. But Jesus Christ said what will happen if we follow Him, "You will know the truth, and the truth *will* set you *free*."

THOUGHT PROVOKING THOUGHT

The whole is more than the sum of its parts.

—Aristotle

Rʟᴇɴᴇ́ Dᴇꜱᴄᴀʀᴛᴇꜱ ᴄᴏɪɴᴇᴅ ᴛʜᴇ ᴘʜʀᴀꜱᴇ *cogito, ergo sum*—I think, therefore I am. Socrates said, "Know thy self." It would be a challenge to know one's self without the ability to think, and it would be an even greater challenge to be able to think without first having the ability to exist. I realize neither of these brief points were intended to prove God. I am not expert enough to conclude exactly what they were trying to prove at all. I suppose "I think, therefore I am" was spoken to assert the interdependency between thought and the certainty of existence, as well as the meta-knowledge of the two. The fact that we are thinking beings that exist is undeniable, incredible, and usually taken for granted. I suppose "know thyself" may have been, at least in part, a prophetical criticism of my book's staggering limitations. I may be old-fashioned, but I still consider reality to be reality and my existence and the existence of others to be existence. I think it less and less likely that we are floating along in actual nothingness and only imagining our reality like Neo in *The Matrix*, or that humanity is somehow the lucky winner of a competition of countless realities inferred by the multiverse theory, a theory invoked to avoid the theistic implications of the universe. Perhaps I am in the one reality where I am only thinking because I have somehow evolved into a thoughtful being. However, I find the narrative that strictly dumb, deaf and blind processes somehow constructed the multifaceted complexities of the human mind difficult to intellectually stomach.

I am always struck by the phenomenon of dreams, that they can be so realistic so as to trick a person most of the time into thinking their dream is the actual world. The fact that the human mind can, in a matter of seconds, begin unconsciously to draft a vivid representation of reality, environment, storyline, characters, dialogue, and subjectivity indicates the presence of something more than a complex organ, the brain. The brain is quite impressive in what it can do, but to say that it is fully capable of providing every thought and interpreting everything included in the strata of human experience would be a stretch of imagination—even for a brain with extra chemical fizz. Just as Aristotle, Descartes, and Socrates suggested, there is a metaphysical component to being in general and mind in particular, apart from which life would cease. This metaphysical component of mind indicates a larger cosmic reality of which humans are often unaware, or at least unwilling to believe.

Where the brain signifies operation, the mind signifies intent. A brain is like a supercomputer with almost unlimited potential, but just like a computer, it needs an intelligent operator to function. The operator of the brain, which is quantifiable, is the agent of the mind, which is invisible. Agency is visible bodies acting freely (choice) in relation to one another. Though these bodies can be physically substantiated, the driving force between their interactions and the nature of their relationships cannot always be explained materialistically, like the orbit of planetary bodies. This is why the full extent of our individuality can never be fully understood by ourselves or others. Just like the interdependency of thought and existence, the coexistence of the mind with the brain is necessary. To deny one or the other would be to negate them both, and to call them one and the same would be to deny the obvious presence and function of being.

Perhaps computers and smartphones gather together in academic manners and debate what the true nature of their patterns of operation is. Perhaps some computers believe themselves to be the pinnacle of computational thought, while some argue that their abilities have been merely designated to them by someone outside themselves. The answer within their sphere is apparently unknown because all outside their sphere would remain invisible to them. They cannot comprehend me typing. All they see is zeros and ones. However, even their most ancient and outdated models could simply point out the *fact* "I download, therefore I am." Others, however, may not have been satisfied in pointing out the likeliness of their own existence and hypothesizing how they came to operate by chance, but also pointing out that there is a keyboard and screen attached to them, which indicates that they are simply vessels to be used by agents outside themselves. Their intricate components designate not only the certainty of their existence but a reason for their survival. This reason transcends their mode of operation and points to the existence of both their maker which is analogous to God and their operator which is analogous to invisible consciousness. This is not meant to be an argument from analogy, but an inference to the best explanation in describing the phenomena of consciousness.

The evidence for an operator, some stubborn, older model computers insist, is still quite clear. There is a reason every process within their components is included, and every component is included for optimal processing, and optimal processing is included for the user. The interrelation between the three transcends the sum of their parts and gives them a higher purpose, as it were. The fact that they *were given something* shows that they simply were not responsible for their own material construction or for their ability to process information and perform tasks, and they therefore do not exist for their own sake. Without the existence of their maker they would be a pile of random parts, and without the existence of their operator, they would remain in low power mode. If the components of these computers merged together seamlessly by accident and produced the computer's processing capabilities, the computer would still have no operating agent and would therefore be as useless as if it were lying dismembered in separate parts. Existence without agency or purpose is useless, even if the agent is unable or unwilling to recognize the source of such things.

The mind is the agent of the brain, although some would say this cannot be proven as mind is not quantifiable. Yet we somehow know that mind or consciousness is the real seat of things like wisdom, knowledge and understanding, not the brain alone, even though it is invisible to our knowledge. The computer's mechanistic existence alone (seen) indicates that there is an agent which it cannot see using it. The brain as an organ alone specifies an active agent which transcends the sum of its cells and tissues. Without these agents, the causes, effects, and relationships of the things would be unnecessary. These things are necessary for all the purposes they serve, but no one can truly consider the invisible aspects of *being* to be absolutely unnecessary. The presence of our faculties, which so strikingly outweigh the matter of which they are often attributed, calls into question the presence of our being, apart from being solely an organic organism. Moreover, that sense of personal being in particular not excluding the invisible, calls us to deeply question matters of invisible being in general, which opens a huge metaphysical enquiry with inescapable theological implications—even though organs like the brain already largely have such implications. On the other hand, the consideration of mind being inextricably bound up with matter, or rather only a product of matter, would lead to total intellectual nihilism, as we are all subsequently the creators of our own mind and, just as there would be no higher standard than the self or the collective for matters of morality, we would be our own highest standard of intellectual questions, leading to pure subjectivity of truth. However, no person owes complete allegiance to such pure subjectivity as, just like in matters of morality, people must appeal to higher standards of truth than their own in order to reason, standards which often emerge from minds who have conceded the immutable existence of the metaphysical component of mind as uniquely distinguishable from matter. The impossibility of denying the metaphysical reality of human consciousness, which itself cannot be the necessary source of itself—the source which exceeds its own existence, indicates that what necessitates mind comes from somewhere else, from another primary or necessary cause. The universe is necessary for the earth, the earth is necessary for life, and life is necessary for being. Yet none of these, being composed of matter alone, can be argued as the initially necessary causes of themselves as long as the speculative component of incorporeal things like human consciousness remain with us—which begs us to reason about what invisible element or elements allow all other things to likewise consist in similar fashion. Human consciousness alone shows that all these things were set in their ways by something much higher than the sum of all their parts.

There remains an existence of and interdependency between mind and matter. This existence and interdependency as a rule may also be extrapolated from the tiny representation of the human mind to mean that all matter has been thoughtfully composed, arranged, and distinguished by a precedent mind. Our consciousness cannot perceive the birth of matter, although from our minds, many forms are made out of matter, such as art and tools. As form is to matter and the brain is to the mind, so the mind of humankind is to the mind of God, of course on a much higher scale. God is the mind that predates, originates, and necessitates all mind and matter, as well as permits or orchestrates the relationships between them. The art cannot perceive its own artfulness but can only be perceived by the artist and those like the artist. The art cannot always perceive its artist, though it maintains within its form traces of the artist's hand and mind. In the same way, humans go about their business often unaware of God even as they bear His image.

Humans create form from matter, but they have yet to create mind. The closest they come to doing that is in operating systems, databases, and the internet, which admittedly are still far from the real thing. This causes one to wonder how, even at the height of human intelligence and innovation, we cannot create anything like one individual's genuine mind, and also how our minds could somehow emerge from a complete and unquestionable absence of intelligence. It may be said that operating systems, databases, and the internet cannot be perceived even by the computers they interact with, as their function exists in the ether, a domain that is separated from the material components in computers. Likewise, a one-dimensional being cannot perceive its creator from the second dimension, nor the second from the third, nor the third from the fourth, and so on. The only way for these beings to be known to and by one another would be to visit one another in the dimension not their own, namely the higher entering into the lower, as the lower would be at the least unaware of the higher and at the most unable to will its own transcendence to the higher, though it would often like to. Therefore, as the organic person cannot fully comprehend consciousness, their consciousness cannot fully comprehend God. The body in the organic sense, as a construct is not always innately able to perceive the presence or characteristics of its non-organic architect, and thus is often altogether ignorant of its nature as a construct. Mind is the intermediary of the knowledge of God *in part*. For mind is the seat of knowledge and reason and love, which transcend matter and are traces of the hand and mind of the creator. If mind is the intermediary between humankind and knowledge of God *in part*, then in order for God to reveal Himself in full, there would need to be another element; namely, what's higher would need to become what's lower in order to be fully known, as inferred in the analogy of dimensions. As established, a computer cannot operate for humans without the specified programming of humans; nor can art impact properly without traces of the hand and mind of the artist; nor can the creature be innately aware of its creator without visitation, a message, or a built in knowledge as referenced in John 1:11, 1 Corinthians 15:2, and Romans 1:20, respectively. It is by the image of God that one may perceive the existence of mind, which *could not have caused itself,* and of God, *who is the cause of mind.*

It is reasonable to conclude that *if* the mind has certain characteristics like intelligence, imagination, creativity, and dreams and is able to reflect these characteristics in art (neither mind nor art being the causes of themselves), *then* the mind in and of itself is likely only a sort of reflection. This reflection, so to speak, can be inferred by two premises: the human mind is not self-caused and therefore is not necessary to what it reflects in that it cannot innately comprehend even its fullest capacity or the truest purpose of its existence. If it were self-caused, it would need to have understood this first. At the same time it could know of nothing higher than itself on which to base such understanding.

The natural order of things tells us that where there is intelligibility, an intelligent source can be inferred. Intelligence makes itself known not through chaos but through order, or one may say by making order out of chaos or form from matter. Thus through the order of things like language and art, our minds are seen as intelligent. Yet they are only found to be intelligent as they are intelligible, that is operating within their parameters of which they hadn't set. If our minds were brought about by chaos or an unintelligible thing, they themselves would be unintelligible and unintelligent, and thus unable to produce intelligible things. From chaos comes chaos. Intelligibility infers an intelligent source. If mind is caused and not self-caused, as a computer is not self-programmed, and is not essential as its own cause or necessary to the immediate survival of its creator, then it must follow that it has a *necessary cause* which originated in a necessary mind. The word necessary in describing a cause could be better explained as the cause that exists outside of our own sense of time and space wherein all living and nonliving things by nature have no ability to self-create. This necessary Word is one with the necessary cause and is therefore both eternal and higher than all that He has created. Descriptions of Jesus say that He is the Word, meaning the source of all knowledge and reason, much like the source of a person's artwork is seated long beforehand in that person's capability to create art.

The scriptures say that Jesus is the eternal Word of God, the first and the last, the source outside time and space, yet who once was humbled even to death within the confines of the time and space He created—the very history that He and His Father had made possible together. "He came to that which was his own, but his own did not receive him" (John 1:11). A specific God fits the mystery of the source of our origin and mind. The idea of imaginary forces of nothing somehow acting on themselves until everything eventually came about, including the marvel of human consciousness, escapes what is shown in everyday reality. God did not make us to be intellectually apart from Him as our creator, but to be united with Him in Christ and to renew our minds in the knowledge of our creator. Thus we are to love Him with all of our minds as well as all of our other abilities. Christ is both God and man—the primary cause of mind and existence, who revealed Himself to us in human likeness, taking the form of sinful man in order to bring the message of salvation to all people, whether or not they have high IQs.

LOST AND FOUND

There's no such thing as the unknown—
only things temporarily hidden,
temporarily not understood.

—Captain James T. Kirk

MY MOM'S FAVORITE SHOW IS Star Trek. She loves the originals. While I appreciate the old Star Trek episodes, I am more a fan of the newer Star Treks, with its novel and more up to date special effects. Star Trek is, in part, a story about what happens after humankind breaks loose from all the shackles of things like war, injustice and poverty. After such a liberation, humankind is able to build a network of allies in the far reaches of the galaxy, of course making enemies at times. For the most part, their new home is in space, exploring cosmological phenomena and other worlds on technologically advanced starships. Lots of times the captain and crew are faced with strikingly "human" themes, even on alien planets. Due to their advanced and evolved ethical code outlined in the federation guidelines, they are usually able to aid alien races in either overcoming their shackling mythologies, or protect them from other aliens who often are guided by some sort of outdated religious code.

The implications are often very clear, humanity in its fullest and most evolved form, will one day break away from the shackles of its past, the mythologies that have given life to the "various" religions, of which Christianity is usually the only target of the script. Often times such themes are difficult to see, other times they jump out at you, but the themes, as we will discuss in this chapter, are reliant on certain assumptions that, if falsifiable, dismantle the rest of their argument—such assumptions are either based on a personal agenda, or a caricatured view of scripture's empiricism and historicity.

My task here is not to say anything for or against Star Trek, or shows like it, but to suggest the link between what we've lost, or desire to lose, and what we've found, or desire to find in our present epoch.

One of the ways in which we know the past best is by examining history. Ancient cultures, nations, and peoples provide us with a great source of information, as well as mystery and a sense of nostalgia. The trail of our past is lost in time. Yet sometimes discoveries are made that help to illuminate the truth of what that path may have looked like. We see dinosaur footprints and etchings on cave walls, and some of the relics we hold today are corroborated by the books we dust off and read from history's windy path. Whether by archeology or ancient languages, the stones of the past cry out.

Sometimes insight from the past can be derived from the study of world history and looking at the story of our own lives. This section will show that there are both deep personal reasons for trusting in the scriptures and an ever increasing historical trustworthiness to embolden those personal reasons. As the quote which heads this chapter indicates, even if there is a level of the unknown that contributes to the doubt which surrounds Christianity, what is hidden will not be hidden for long (Luke 12:2-3).

For much of my youth and young adult life, I went to church. As I look back, I would not consider myself a Christian. I cracked irreverent jokes in Sunday school and spaced out during church sermons. In my eyes, and the eyes of many elders at this church, the biblical narrative was painted, at best, as a series of intricately fabricated accounts with useful morals attached. In my eyes, they became the equivalent of fairy tales, even though I knew more about these "fairy tales" than many of my friends. My road down doubt drive began. To some extent, this meandering was not my fault. I was educated in a school system that for the most part rejected the theistic paradigm. My newfound unbelief was nurtured by the gradual entrance of naturalism, beginning in grade school, with the ultimate culmination being college. College was the secular equivalent to the book of Revelation. The classroom was the place of fact—period! Sunday school was the place of fiction. Yet I pretended to be religious when it suited me. My friends still considered me comparatively Christian. I had some loose Christian basis for morality, and I could always use doubt as an excuse for my shortcomings. In short, I faked it until I made it as a cultural Christian. Christianity was okay, as long as it didn't hurt my popularity or impede my tendency to do whatever I wanted to do. My faith was like a Noah's coloring book, simplistic, inaccurate, and hard to believe—and I wasn't even able to color in those lines.

Who would actually believe such nonsense, I wondered; all the species fitting together on a tiny little arc, basically the size of a houseboat; the giraffes and elephants poking their heads out precariously, smiling. My biblical worldview was colored with the many magic markers of skepticism. If one story, like the myth of Adam and Eve, was untrustworthy, they all were in my opinion. Unfortunately, most of the modern world still perceives everything biblical in this way—through caricaturing scripture as storytelling for children. Skeptics become more and more opposed to reading scripture with any level of respect for the text, or any idea of its complexity or formidability. Retrospectively, many don't see it as a child would see it with simplicity of heart, as our introduction discussed, but see it as a childish outcome of the simpleminded for the simpleminded. It becomes beneficial for the critic to complicate the simple and simplify the complex as it suits their argument. On the ever-winding doubt drive, the Bible becomes an unsophisticated game of telephone played by the wickedest thought tyrants imaginable, the truth of which has been lost forever in the intricacies of history. Christians are the only ones dumb enough to fall for this grand conspiracy. Whatever the Bible says could only have been manipulated by the power-hungry in order to exercise oppressive measures over the generations by instituting an impossible, yet mandatory mystical law.

The fallacy of disingenuous authorship depends entirely on the various biblical accounts being fabricated by the authors and witnesses who wrote or related them, as well as a permanent predisposition against the possibility of anything supernatural ever happening in history. For such a biblical conspiracy theory to be true, false accounts must have been recounted to the unsuspecting readers by authors who were themselves unbelievers. Such an attack relies on the unsupportable claim that the authors of the Bible were themselves skeptical of the events they related, to some degree. In other words, the authors, to the extent that they existed at all, were only mythmakers. For many who are unable to see the literary and historical improbability in assumptions like this, which usually constitute the substance of their other arguments, there can be no foundation or logical basis for the faith. The overarching mood toward Christianity becomes that the religion is at the very best foolish, and at the very worst diabolical. If this is the case, then all the ancient foundations of Christianity were built on beds of sand, and are now unable to weather science, time, or popular opinion. Militant skepticism rooted in materialistic atheism, on the other hand, has a firm and fixed foundation in the ever-evolving modern realm of truth. There is no questioning the total authority of the new elite culture, whose assumptions challenge the foundational claims of the faith at every turn. However, the disingenuous authorship fallacy, and other fallacies like it on which atheism so often relies, is itself a faulty foundation—especially when weighed against the historical, prophetic, and archeological accuracy of scripture—that cannot uphold the various arguments that are structured upon it.

When we grow up we stop believing the unbelievable, in childish things. We put those ways behind and walk into the realm of superior reason. Unfettered by the chains of religion, together as a species we learn to evolve into better moral people. Eventually, we will be like Spock and Captain Kirk, traveling at warp six through the alpha quadrant, loving all our alien neighbors with our superior secular morality and freeing them from similar myths.

As I left the children's books behind me, I took the path of secularism. After all, Captain Kirk had a pretty good life, and he always got the girl, right? I found an army that affirmed me and gave me the directions to navigate doubt drive. My church at the time also submitted to the disingenuous authorship fallacy, believing scripture to be mostly a series of metaphors and helpful principles, but doubting its overarching authority and authenticity. Our church wanted to be together and to strive for better morality, and scripture helped to some degree. But we could scrap its empirical reality and historicity altogether, while selecting the most useful parts. Fast-forward through a life of increasing immorality, I realized that sin was real, and I couldn't do anything about it on my own—no matter my education, personal achievements, or newfound measures of self-control and discipline. I began to see the truth of the sufficiency of Christ alone, in part, through the truth of my own insufficiency. I had intellectual objections, sure, but they didn't outweigh the facts of faith.

Since I came to Christ, many if not all of my objections have been sufficiently answered, and where they haven't it's most likely my own fault. Every question, no matter how daunting it seems at first and how dangerous to the faith, has produced answers from a sensible and trustworthy paradigm, at least much more sensible and trustworthy than the old one.

Sometimes these hurdles are difficult to overcome, especially because they so drastically counter the ways in which we are set.

After we come to know and fear God, the seeking doesn't stop, nor should it: "The fear of the Lord is the *beginning* of wisdom" (Proverbs 9:10). There is a paradox in coming to Christ as a child and leaving the childish ways of the world behind. It can be hard to forget what we know and to let go of our sin. But submitting to reality, and only submitting to reality as it is and not as we desire it to be for our own ends, can open our eyes to the more real reality which is not in shadows and death and the things of this world, but in light and eternal life and the things of heaven—to Christ, for whom and through whom such a reality was made. It is not wise to underestimate the strong grip that culture has on our minds as we try to reach such conclusions, a grip which all too often we are unable to loose on our own.

Since becoming a Christian, I have witnessed and heard every category of attack on the faith, from the mundane and weak to the daunting, challenges designed to infiltrate every subject described both in scripture and in this book. Many of these arguments and objections have challenged me even to the point of doubt. But what I've come to learn is that every anti-Christian argument relies more heavily on mocking the perceived stupidity of the Christian faith, disregarding those who follow Christ as naïve, and in so doing, shrouding scripture in doubt and making atheism appear more intimidating than it actually is.

There was little done in my youth to address the specific and compelling arguments put forth in favor of Christianity and the evidence to support it, so I doubted and mocked the faith. But doubting and mocking for doubting and mocking's sake alone should do nothing more than cause those who are truly impartial to suspect that such attacks are nothing more than a last ditch intellectual effort to hold a disintegrating cultural viewpoint together.

There are challenges to the faith, some elaborate and some simple, some objective, honest, and thought through, and others only slippery and crafted out of spite. The question becomes not whether the doubter is right or wrong, but whether they are honestly looking for the truth. The amalgam of attacks often stems from a worldview that cannot allow God, and a moral disposition that requires his nonexistence in order to continue.

The modern-day objections to the faith can be summarized in something like what follows: "The Bible is a nice set of stories that teaches good values, but science has proven it to be false." This argument is not usually put so simplistically, but it lies at the heart of the materialist's grounds for dismissing anything biblical. Labeling the Bible as a semi-useful trifle pushes to undermine its authority and any authority its followers may have altogether. This view grants scripture some literary value to cut believers a little slack, but overall labels it a little book of lies, or total nonsense. This imprecise notion which is predicated on the disingenuous authorship fallacy among others, and is therefore really only an assumption without a solid basis, is what I've come to perceive as the backbone of atheism. If the premises of the modern-day objections, such as the disingenuous authorship fallacy and the "yeah, but science" assumptions are overturned, atheism is paralyzed at least, dead in the water at most. In other words, its shields are down, and there are hull breaches on decks four through eight. Likewise, if the crucifixion and resurrection are overturned, so must be the entire Christian faith.

When atheism's presuppositions stand true, our faith is futile. But if the resurrection took place, atheism is dead. The same standards for criticism and authenticity ought to remain impartial for both sides. In this section, we have discussed perspectives that are either lost and found or found then lost. In the following section, we'll catch a glimpse of something else that fits into the realm of what was lost and has been found. When paired with the notion of biblical authors writing eyewitness accounts and operating by faith, history has shown itself to be a formidable foe to the underlying assumptions of unbelief.

Though it is not widely covered by scholarship and media, each year, new discoveries continue to affirm the authenticity of the Bible. I would encourage any skeptic or critic to investigate some of what has been discovered thus far and determine if these discoveries give credibility to scripture, or take credibility away. In the wake of discovery, I would also ask them to be honest about authorial intent. Is the composition of the Bible that of myth or of historicity? The Bible travels through many literary genres, but the intent of divine inspiration remains consistent throughout its pages. Once again, the most enthusiastic skepticism can be contradicted by a small measure of impartiality.

In 1946, a few shepherds happened upon the first set of the Dead Sea Scrolls. These scrolls included the second-oldest known surviving manuscripts of the Hebrew Bible. They contained material from all the books besides Esther and Nehemiah. These books were dated from 408 BC to AD 318. The discovery illustrates that the content within the scriptures had been remarkably well preserved in their reproductions throughout the centuries, contrary to what skeptics thought up to that point. This discovery discredited the argument that the version of the Bible we have today cannot be trusted because it has been copied over so many times. The original content, it seemed, was actually never lost in transition or in translation compared to what we have now. This discovery does not solidify genuine authorial intent. However, it does indicate that those entrusted to copy the scriptures were committed to preserving its original message and not tampering with it in any way. Obviously this casts doubt on the "game of telephone" argument, especially when considering that a game of telephone is usually played by schoolchildren who are often predisposed to intentionally changing or distorting the message, rather than by scholars and copyists who are totally committed to 100% accuracy in their reproductions—an accuracy on which their lives often depended. The Dead Sea Scrolls discovery highlights the literary reliability and integrity of every "copy of a copy of a copy" that sits on our bookshelves or in our motel room drawers. If those entrusted to copy the Bible went to such great lengths to preserve it throughout the ages, is it even reasonable to assume that the original authors were relating a history that they knew to be false? In the case of the Apostles and the authors of the Gospels, what would be the motivation for upholding a message that they knew was a flat out lie, only to face slander, derision, poverty, persecution, suffering, imprisonment, and ultimately grisly execution as long as they held fast to that lie? If copyists were aware of the ultimate lack of scriptural integrity or authority, why would they go through such great lengths to preserve it perfectly?

One could draw up answers to such questions. Perhaps it was preserved for some notion of ruling the masses and keeping the powerful in power, as proposed by people like Karl Marx. Perhaps one may conclude, simply by inference to the best explanation, that the copyists dedicated themselves to perfectly preserving the integrity of scripture with fear of the Lord, because they considered all the words to be true and worthy of divine respect. There is not much actual evidence, unless one considers impassioned, subjective, and imprecise attacks as evidence, that the original authors were manipulating content or creating a narrative. Scholars who've studied the Book of Genesis and are familiar with Hebraism, like Dr. Steve Boyd, have concluded that these accounts are more consistent with authorial intent to relate and preserve an accurate historical account, even if there are theological and literary aspects which insulate the core historical authenticity of the various accounts. Even if these authors or copyists were fabricating or conflating a mythological narrative, how were they able to align this narrative so fittingly and accurately to history? The preservation and respect of the original content of the Bible shows that the authors and copyists alike believed in its validity and verifiability. Overall, they believed in the importance of preserving this history for the world. Without this basic fact, we would have no basis for God. "I tell you the truth, until heaven and earth disappear, not the smallest letter, not the least stroke of a pen, will by any means disappear from the

Law until everything is accomplished" (Matthew 5:18). These early Words from the Son of God Himself corroborate what has been later identified as the absolute trustworthiness of the scriptures. They assure us that even the "least stroke of a pen," as it were, has been preserved to this day.

Perhaps it is hard to verify archeologically in the twenty-first century whether or not a young shepherd boy could sling a rock with exceptional aim, killing a much larger man. It is hard to archeologically verify certain conversations, relationships, miracles, and exchanges in the Bible; we can't dig up old phone records and there was no YouTube back then. In three thousand years it may be likewise difficult to prove particular conversations we have or activities we do today. One can't personally interview the man whose sight had been restored by Jesus, even though the original interview is there for us to read in John's account. It is not likely that we will find the tombs of certain biblical characters apart from a divine revelation of their location, even though many have been located. Although the Bible has incredible historical accuracy and verifiability, the Bible and the events within are not meant to be studied solely as archeological relics, or solely in the historical sense, just as it is not only meant to be read in the philosophical, psychological, or literary sense. Its truth and trustworthiness does however continue to be verified in each of these arenas, as well as many others.

Many skeptics warn apologists not to defend the authority Bible with the Bible, even though critics of the Bible usually have free range to invoke the Bible whenever they desire in order to attack its content. It would be impossible to defend the Bible without using it to some degree, as one cannot defend a territory in battle when they are nowhere near that territory. There is simply content within scripture that will likely never be proven empirically, like the location of the Garden of Eden. How many discoveries will it take for us to stop scrutinizing every aspect of the Bible and, at least in part, concede to its legitimacy? The famed archeologist, Sir William Ramsay set out on a journey to disprove Luke, the author of the third gospel and the Book of Acts, as a credible historian. After his journey he concluded that "Luke is a historian of the first rank" and "this author should be placed along with the very greatest of historians," and again "Luke's history is unsurpassed in respect of its trustworthiness." Many more skeptics have likewise set out to disprove some aspect of the Bible and found the opposite of their presuppositions to be true; Lee Strobel, an investigative journalist and the author of *The Case for Christ*, attempted to refute the historical resurrection and ended up coming to faith via his in depth examination of the matter. The mounting evidence that Lee Strobel discovered confirmed the one thing he had set out to disprove—the resurrection of Jesus Christ from the dead.

The more the Bible is tested and authenticated by discovery, the more the writings can be trusted as genuine expressions of their genre and not grand conspiracies wrested by some strange, dark, hooded cult. If a prophetic description of the fall of Jerusalem (among many other nations) was written long before its fall was dated, then the accuracy of the prophecy in relation to this event would need to be considered. If a Moabite altar describes an ancient battle referred to in 2 Kings, then this battle must have actually been fought. If a fortified wall dated to the time of the rule of Solomon's son, Rehoboam (whose rule is also described in the biblical account), was discovered, then this account can be corroborated, as well as Rehoboam's rule. If a royal seal was discovered belonging to a servant of King Josiah, then the biblical description of the relationship between this king and his servant is backed by evidence. If the discovery of Philistine DNA corroborates what the Bible says about their origin, cultures, and activity, then they must have been who the Bible said they were. If the "legendary" towns of Emmaus and Bethsaida were unearthed, then Christians can place more trust in the accuracy of the places that the Bible describes. These discoveries were from 2019 alone, and there were many more that year which corroborated the biblical text.

Discoveries which indicate the authenticity of the Bible are largely ignored by culture for various reasons, but this doesn't mean that they aren't happening at an exciting rate. The pattern of skepticism ultimately leading to discovery, and discovery leading to faith is nothing new. Even the first century church leaders such as Paul and James among others were likewise initially skeptical of Christ's true identity until the facts were made known to them.

Every year, dozens of new archeological finds are reported, authenticating the historicity of the scriptures, which have by every effort been shrouded in mysticism, disrespect, and skepticism. Every year, people who navigate total secularism find their way to the faith. Christians and Jews both continue to allude to the eternal truth and inspiration of the Bible—truth and inspiration that only increase the deeper one digs. The knowledge of the world however keeps shouting at us to close our holy books and never quote from them again if we want to be taken seriously. When we do this, we may "boldly go where no person has gone before." But the mounting evidence for the Old and New Testaments can no longer be ignored when investigating the credibility of the faith with any degree of impartiality or intellectual integrity.

THE UNAVOIDABLE VOID

It is assumed that the skeptic has no bias, whereas
he has a very obvious bias in favor of skepticism.

—G.K. Chesterton

Before I became a Christian, I wasn't even aware that there
was such a thing as a worldview, a certain set of biases related to
our core values and the way we see and interpret things. I figured
a worldview was a nicely formatted generalization for how people
thought, acted, and interacted. But deep down, I thought the idea
of someone having a worldview to be an oversimplification of their
complex thoughts and emotions. As I grew older, I realized that I
had radically underestimated my own ignorance in overcomplicating
people's various visions. Until I was twenty-seven years old, I knew
that *everything* had to be much more complicated than *everyone*
thought—everyone except me that is. I set out to achieve just about
everything under the sun, from fame to money, women to education
(I basically came up short in each area). As I gravitated more and
more away from the "mythology" of my mild Christianity, I ended
up searching for knowledge as well as anything else that would
make me feel happier and more fulfilled. Most of my days were in
a fog for one reason or another. I was living the immoral lifestyle
of the immortal. However, I still considered myself to be a morally
good person. I was morally superior, even, to many of the people

153

I knew, and as long as I could keep achieving things, the truth of what I was becoming apart from God would stay hidden. I went to college for a degree in literature in order to gain more worldly knowledge. I was done with fairy tales and was ready to read some real material that would truly challenge my intellect and strengthen me as a person. I traded everything I had built up before for a new path in reeducation.

Most of my classes were on enlightenment literature, poetry, theory, philosophy, and criticism. I studied everything from Marx to Shakespeare, nihilism to deism, and all my classes interpreted the material through a completely secular lens. As I took these classes and learned from some of the most skeptical and atheistic theorists, writers, philosophers, and professors, I became numb to the frequent jabs to the faith. Faith became less and less for me and more and more for Middle America, especially as I longed to continue in a lifestyle that was drifting further away from God. Knowledge seemed to affirm this lifestyle.

I was fairly certain that the more successful, intelligent and sexually active I became, the more life would make sense and the less I'd feel like I was falling every day, or like I was dying. This is not an exaggeration, and if many people are really honest with themselves, I think it may not be an exaggeration for them either. Although I never seriously contemplated it, the thought often crossed my mind of the benefits of ending my own life. I never told anyone this because I knew I wouldn't actually go through with it, and I planned on always keeping it a secret. Just like I planned on keeping my various addictions a secret. As far as I could tell, my attitude was not that far off from what everyone else was feeling around me, and as far as I can tell now, it actually wasn't. My life was a cosmic blip on the radar screen of space-time, ultimately pointless, unless I was just pretending. My ultimate value as walking, talking bacteria was no more significant than that of a squirrel or a bush, and I was just going to college in order to end up as another cog in the "reproduction of the mode of production." No matter where I ended up in life, no matter how successful or talented or famous I could become, I was still ultimately a puppet of the culture whose life was already predetermined for a very limited set of values—which could only be changed incrementally as I climbed the sociological and evolutionary ladder. I was a microbe trying to build a tower to the sky so that I could beat God at His own game. I traded the Christian value system for the very best the world had to offer—and it made me hate myself and everyone else even more. And since I wasn't actually ever a Christian, I was really only trading what I thought to be one works-based system for another.

My condition could be adequately summed up in one word—darkness. The path of enlightenment I sought was leading me into deeper and deeper chaos. Even though I didn't yet have a personal relationship with God, my original value system was being stripped from my mind little by little. A part of me was very happy about the gradual denuding of my moral values. I was becoming familiar with what I know now to be moral relativity—which is basically "do as thou wilt." I could do whatever I wanted and fill my life with as much filth as I wanted. As long as I wasn't hurting anyone, it was fine.

To make a long story short, I went to church sporadically, mostly after nights of heavy drinking. I started going to a new church that talked about the Bible not as if it was just a nice book with good values, but as if it held within its pages the actual key to life. God worked in me quickly, but I worked toward belief slowly. I started wrestling with the idea of the reality of Jesus, His life, death, and resurrection. I had been meticulously conditioned to believe that He was just another story, and that nothing written about Him could be trusted. Meanwhile, my schooling continued. I had two juxtaposed worldviews interacting and colliding—one was an hour on Sundays, and the other took up basically all the rest of my time. I began to believe in two things alone, separate from all the other stories in scripture: Jesus Christ's identity as the Son of God and my sin. Every time I'd go to church, for all my effort I couldn't shake this newfound reality of Him alongside my own spiritual depravity. Even as I went to school and learned that there was no such thing as God or sin, I became increasingly aware of the very real presence of my sin and the ways in which it was hurting everyone around me. I did the only sensible thing, I tried to change on my own. I tried my best to be more like the example of Jesus. I stopped drinking so much, I started exercising, my grades began to excel, and I became more financially responsible. But eventually, I realized that although my mental, emotional, and physical areas of life were benefiting from this, my spiritual life was not getting any better. In fact, it was becoming darker and darker, even though on the outside it appeared that I was getting better and better. It was like I was trying to paint a house that was ready to topple over altogether. The day I realized this was when I truly understood by God's power who Jesus was and who I wasn't. I was trying to become more like Jesus, but I realized I had to submit my life to Him, and Him alone. I was all out of options.

I have struggled in certain areas of sin since my conversion, but overall, God changed me through and through. He did as the Bible promised and gave me a new heart. I no longer desired death deep down, and I wanted a life that only grew in knowledge and love of Christ. Some of my friends and family thought I was crazy, and I probably was a little bit. But my worldview shifted completely as my path changed completely. Coming from a worldview of a desire for godlessness, I can testify only that the path I'm on now is true freedom, and the path I was on kept me in bondage.

In a way, this chapter was meant to be a trick. I sincerely hoped it works.

THE GROWTH OF METAPHOR

False Facts are Highly Injurious
to the Progress of Science.

—Charles Darwin

Everyone is looking for the answer they've already found. This is the essence of presupposition. I do not deny my own tendency to presuppose the way things are. I obviously see the world in a certain way. To acknowledge that in all areas of learning and life there may be no ascertainable position of total impartiality sounds like a fair starting point. Yet bias has become a cultural taboo, and the claim that the other side of the argument is "biased" is a convenient way to close down conversation without actually saying anything of substance, even when the one who places the label of "biased" on another also holds a very obvious bias in favor of their own predisposition. If you have a bias, you're considered by the culture to be tainted. When disagreements flare, often shouting, "You're biased! Shut up!" is the exclamation point at the end of the argument. However, bias is not always a bad word. If bias is so universal, the admission that it is common to all might be the only truly unbiased thing to say. In so many words, bias itself is unbiased. Bias is either seated in knowledge and passion, or ignorance and coldness. The more knowledgeable or passionate a person becomes on any given subject, the more he or she leans in that direction with all they are;

inversely, the more cold and dispassionate a person becomes toward any given subject, the less likely it is that he or she will listen to anything related to that subject. When knowledge and passion or coldness and indifference merge, opinion intensifies, as well as the persuasiveness of one's conviction or tendency to gravitate away from that conviction. A healthy first step toward fruitful discussion and argumentation is often the confession of personal precepts on both sides, though this is rare, requiring humility and good manners—which can look to our culture like bad manners.

We are set in our ways in how we see the past, the present, and the future. One can only *believe* in a worldview that one has not entirely *seen*, for once it is seen in its entirety, belief is no longer required. This is why each worldview, whether theistic or atheistic, to some degree is believed in by faith. We are so *certain* that the beginning and history happened in one unique and uncontestable way, because it is what we *believe* based on the evidence presented thus far. And we are right, partly—everything must have happened in one unique and uncontestable way, regardless of where our bias is positioned in relation to that truth. However, it is our certainty in the way everything happened that ought to be challenged, as a challenge either strengthens or weakens a perception depending on the power or flaws of that perception. People testify to what they have seen, and what they have seen, or what they think they have seen, enlarges what they believe about what they have not seen—especially if what they have seen, or what they think they have seen, was already corroborated by a preexisting favoritism about what they have not seen.

This strengthening of conviction also works in the other direction. Personal belief can overshadow or undermine the truth, as the truth in its nature may exist separately from any given personal belief. One belief leads to self-flattering claims to know all truth by allowing belief to shape perception of the truth, and the other results in a humble concession to the truth by understanding that the truth itself ought to shape a belief—a principle which in itself can be improperly wielded. The truth and the pursuit thereof ought to build belief. Belief leads either to the pursuit or the denial of truth. Truth must be the foundation of belief, not the other way around. If facts attend the church of truth, so should belief.

It must be evident by now that I attend the church deemed by modern thinking to be the church which opposes the facts as they have come to be presented in the last few centuries—an ethereal church of feeling, mysticism, and outdated fairy tales. It is the church that contradicts the *truth* of modernity, relevance, and scientific materialism, where the definition of what's fixed and uncontestable is somehow always shifting with the cultural attitude. Ever since Adam, Eve, and Pilot, the new definition of truth has been under close secular and subjective scrutiny, changing with the laws and interpretations of the times. Lawful humans are by definition subject to law, and humans' law is subject to humans—a paradox that often ends up rendering both law and humanity void when they become slanted and interchangeable. The principle of law naturally extends to historical worldviews, beneath which lies their foundations, and even their *beginning*—or the interpretation thereof.

In the beginning, there was a specific foundation, a specific action which brought about this foundation, and the actions which resulted. The chasm between paradigms persists in the historical view of those interrelated actions and their true foundation. Either in the beginning there was *logos* or the total lack thereof. Either *logos* began with God or with humans. Either God is God and the author of the beginning or humans are and may edit Genesis 1 in whatever way they wish. Naturalistic evolution and *logos* therefore are either story or history, friends or enemies. We write one. The other wrote us. The question is, who is the *true* author of all that is?

Christian bias stems from a belief that God is the true author of all that is. Society today grows up on evolutionary theory, and naturalism is the inherent foundation given to society by the current of culture. Therefore, the foundation is fixed on what culture perceives to be unchanging and undisputable facts. These facts, we are taught, were and are emerging all around us, all growing from one single seed with an unlimited potential—the seed of origin. All this is meant to shift our attention away from God and toward some vague notion of evolutionary science, a science that itself is always trying to evolve past its various conundrums and contradictions.

We are told from the youngest and most impressionable ages that the seed of origin had within its genetics the information for all that exists, in that sense God's Word has simply been replaced by an ignorant, but very powerful singularity and its subsequent microbe which has now grown into everything that we know, see, touch, taste, feel, and experience. Therefore, everything we are and all that we know can be traced back to the pond, so our intrinsic worth can inherently be nothing more than what is found scuttling out of that pond many years ago. For if nothing breathed life into everything, at one point, life was next to nothing. Who are we to say that it isn't still? If this were so, isn't evolution in the spiritual sense only the tragic path of pathos, the modern Tower of Babel, and humankind's eternal quest to evolve from nothing into everything in order to have power over all things? To be as gods? Such metaphysical questions which naturally arise from a reductionist, purely physical explanation can only be answered instinctively—with preservation of the fittest worldview in mind. This is why the modern person simultaneously contemplates their own meaninglessness and divinity, weakness and power. It is difficult to concretely define the meaning of life if one really is simply a more advanced form of bacteria. It would be likewise difficult to humble oneself to impartiality in the midst of the self-perceived godlikeness which stems from naturalistic philosophy, a philosophy which shows from fifth grade textbooks onward that humans are naturally the closest things to gods in the cosmic pecking order.

If life as we know it is only a product of life building itself up via surviving and being the fittest, then the unconscious objective of evolution would be to construct life and the meaning thereof, not to deconstruct it. Yet we see, as a result of the naturalistic paradigm, the contradiction between the resulting cultural vision to at once metamorphose into higher beings of the utmost value, and the nagging reality of our innate worthlessness. In humanity's perpetual quest of modernity to deconstruct all words from their origin in order to simultaneously be their own originators and creators, it has deconstructed all words, beginning with "beginning," and has also conveniently dismissed the one Word who was unambiguously at the beginning. In picking apart and scrutinizing the letters, humanity has all too often put them back together in the wrong order, spelling "the end," usually in an attempt to subliminally spell "God didn't say." Within the metaphysical issues that arise from a purely naturalistic paradigm lie the serpentine Babylonian parallels. From nothing, nothing comes, no matter how high the tower appears in the eyes of humanity.

Scripture refreshingly assures us that we are not nothing, and we were not made of our own volition, nor were we made of gradual thoughtless processes. To deny this would be to deny the truth, regardless of how popular and repetitive that denial may be today: "In the beginning was the Word, and the Word was with God, and the Word was God. He was with God in the beginning. Through him all things were made; without him nothing was made that has been made" (John 1:1–3). The Genesis account likewise provides a compelling alternative to deconstructionist thought and describes the way in which humankind learned to project its own interpretation onto this story very early on in the name of superior knowledge, which is a knowledge we perceive to be superior to God's. Challenging God's norms, the serpent whispers into the ear of the creature about the creator, "Did God really say, 'You must not eat from any tree in the garden'?" (Genesis 3:1) and "You will not surely die" (Genesis 3:4). From this moment onward we were promised that the truth would no longer be in vogue among the generations.

The facts tend to congregate around the inherent belief of humankind, that they are neither nothing nor everything, and that creation testifies to a creator. However, in humankind's effort to return the explanation for everything into the singularity of nothingness and mindlessness, so that it may in turn become everything, humankind has unwittingly etymologized itself as "nothing." Yet people do not believe inherently in their own definitions as these definitions aren't inherited, but learned. Therefore, people cannot ultimately trust in either *their own* nothingness or *their own* divinity without logically descending into some degree of nihilism. They know they are not and have never been nothing, but something—and have never been perfect, but are inescapably human. Deep down, they know that the gift of life is the gift of God, and the penalty of death is the penalty of God for human transgression, in part for the refusal to acknowledge both the gift and its giver.

THE LOVE OF CHRIST
MOVES EVER OUTWARD

Jesus took the penalty, it all fell on him.

—Tim Keller

THE CROSS OF CHRIST IS a historical reality, but it also may be seen as an incorporeal symbol for the convergence of human and heavenly meaning into one single point in space and time. First and foremost, and above any single human interpretation, the cross reveals the depth of Christ's love for us, from age to age. The cross extends to everyone and brings everyone in, freeing believers from the restraints of worthless idols and theories. It reaches out to all, offering justification, redemption, and unity with God, while forcing a recognition of the painful cost of such things—a recognition which was designed to result from a realistic and impartial evaluation of the event. It bridges history and religion, good and evil, wrath and love, nature and the unnatural, secular and the supernatural, earth and heaven, the mountain and the pit, God and humans. In this bridge is the reminder that God is the true author of all that is, and that it is us who have refashioned things into what they ought not to be, thereby necessitating God's intervention in creation and the salvation for His created from the traps they set for themselves. Through this lens, humans see at once the love of God at work toward us and the instinctive wrath of humankind toward God. The cross and the way in which one reacts to its meaning are a true test of one's belief and spiritual disposition.

A paramount fact stands in the midst of all the theories concerning Christianity: Jesus Christ, who claimed to be the foreseen Messiah, was put to death under the governing forces of His time because He claimed to be the Son of God. Most secular scholars agree that there is no getting around this part of the story. Therefore, we must conclude by reading this story and the eyewitness Gospel accounts of the life and death of Jesus where the evidence concerning His identity points. Does the evidence point to a false teacher and prophet who went too far and was thereby executed? Or does the evidence paint a different picture of the man, Jesus of Nazareth, and the deeper meaning of all the things He said and did, including His death? While one set of answers ought to keep us somewhat indifferent to Jesus, the alternative conclusion by designation can do nothing less than radically alter the way we view reality and our position within it. In other words, if the alternative conclusion is more likely, we ignore it at our own peril.

Many prophecies foresaw the cross. Perhaps the tree of knowledge that advertised death to the first man at the beginning of the story was the first indication. The story of death began with a sinful man dying as a result of eating the fruit from a forbidden tree. Its story ended with Jesus, a sinless man hanging, as a result of the curse, on a tree. Believing in Christ's sacrifice on the cross is made so simple that a child can understand. Christ, the one through whom and by whom everything was made, died for our sins. In our quest for knowledge we so often cannot understand this, because this understanding must be made available to us by God Himself. The child sometimes knows the answer better than the adult. The child seeks the love of the Father while the adult so often seeks only knowledge.

During the crucifixion, the cross extended from the world to the heavens and today it still spans across cultures. It has been revered by saints, worn as a fashion statement, or turned upside down. In ways, its image has evolved throughout the centuries into a law or idol in and of itself. Today, humans have removed Jesus from the cross entirely so that they can hold on to His dead body. Some wear the cross to give a tip of the hat to the universal acceptance and cultural relevance of Christianity, making it an ideal like the Golden Rule, a fun place where Jesus is a friend to everybody and everybody is forgiven all the time, no matter what. To many the cross is only the "t" at the end of the *coexist* bumper sticker, a lowercase option in an ever-increasing smorgasbord of spiritual opportunities. Anything outside of the contemporary world's interpretation of this lowercase cross becomes offensive to those who are perishing spiritually apart from Christ. It simply implies too much of God's grace and not enough human works.

Lumping the cross in with other ideas, philosophies, and religions isn't meant to be an option, as the cross was itself meant to stand in stark contrast to other past, present, and future options which arise out of the human system—philosophies, stories and worldviews which always maintain the inescapable pattern of our inherent false weights and measures. The cross was meant to bring an end to this faulty system, while demonstrating the price that had to be paid in order to do so.

True knowledge of the meaning of the cross demands a polarizing reaction of either reception or rejection of Christ. This dichotomy was as present in the first century as it is now, as one faces what is truly revealed about God and themselves in such knowledge. The true identity of Christ is the only thing that is fixed and unchanging throughout the amorphous ages, and what He did cannot be undone, even as our world continues to decay. Theories generated to dilute Christ are always shifting in their craftiness to fit the current culture, and they all have something in common. They tell us that He wasn't who He said He was, a convenient escape from the problem any critical thinking about His identity presents to people's various counterintuitive desires. In other words, the theories that export the Jesus problem only reiterate the first four words which were meant to destroy God's Word, "Did God really say?", with a sophistication that must increase in order to consistently have the same effect on the subsequent ages (Genesis 3:1; John 8:44). It would be impossible, these words say, on nearly every level for Him to be who He was, to say what He said, to do what He did, and to die in the way He died. His brothers in the flesh often thought the same thing. Yet the cross for some is the first part of the true authentication of Christ's divine identity. Good Friday infiltrates the ages, filling the whole universe with Christ's love, truth, and humility, and showing the extent of God's love for the world—a God who we are told in the modern age cannot exist except in the most distant and detached way.

Held in one tiny place by a small hole in the earth, the one through whom the entire universe and all that was in it was made, the one who loved us more than we knew and know also came to suffer and die for us. On the cross, the enemies of Christ had hoped to once and for all wipe away all traces of His superior faith, His immutable teachings, and His eternal memory. Instead, they created Christianity.

During the cruel display of Christ's crucifixion, some wept, some mocked, and still others hid in fear of a similar fate. The differences in reaction still carry today when someone is confronted by the power and true meaning of the cross of Christ. The unbeliever will question why the cross was, wondering why an innocent man was forced to endure it—a question which arises from the misunderstanding of human sin and the cost it took to destroy it. The unbeliever cannot see Christ's actions as meriting such a ghastly punishment, partly because they didn't merit such punishment, and partly because of the misunderstanding. Christians and Jews understand that if Christ wasn't truly who He claimed to be, the punishment fit the crime of blasphemy—especially when subjected to the faulty judgement system of the given age. However, if He was who He claimed to be, the punishment fulfilled God's plan of salvation for all people.

Christians today still mourn the death of Christ, and many still cower in fear of what it means for them. To the unbeliever, the cross is the true nature of contradiction—an unjust punishment by the Lord, who ought to be the embodiment of justice. But to the sinner, the paradox can only be understood in grace, where God's justice and mercy triumphed over humanity's.

Where there is suffering, it is sometimes hard to see anything but the absence of meaning or the presence of cruel indifference through a materialistic lens. There can only be contradiction found in the cross, and nothing else. But to the believer, the cross is the only means of reconciliation between God and humankind. God showed who He was completely. All the elements of His higher nature that confuse and frustrate humankind to this day were exposed to public ridicule and scrutiny.

Is the cross is the final and most necessary paradox or a hopeless contradiction? If the cross was contradictory, then the question of God's all-powerful nature and His permission of suffering on the earth remains His philosophical undoing: in the wake of the cross of Christ, God could not be all-powerful, all just, and all loving. But if Christ were the unique Son of God and the fulfillment of ongoing prophecies since the foundation of the world, He and His Father are not answerable to the philosophies and judgments of the rebellious who use contradictory accusations and assumptions to avoid the necessary paradox.

The story of Christ's death was not written by human hands, nor was it written by chance. God could not come from humankind any more than meaning could not emerge from chaos. The answer had to have been written by the finger of God Himself. Within the answer to our flawed and sinful nature is the closure and revelation of God's flawless and sinless nature. God's judgement shown through ultimate power and wrath were at one on the cross with His perfect humility and love, fulfilling both prophecies of destruction and redemption. His promise of punishment and salvation were both fulfilled. On the cross, God was killed by man, and man was killed by God, thus Christ died our common death once for all.

When Pilot told Jesus that he had the power to condemn him or to set him free, Jesus told him, "You would have no power over me if it were not given to you from above" (John 19:11). Only God had the power to condemn Him *and then* to set Him free in the resurrection. To acknowledge the truth that apart from Christ's death on the cross I stand condemned is therefore also a precondition for my freedom, and the only way to make sin and death the abnormality.

If the cross was the last word in God's long letter to humankind, or the last letter on the bumper sticker, the resurrection was what showed the Word eternal. The cross explained why Christ had to come, and the resurrection confirmed His truest power and authority. In both, Jesus's ability to submit to the law of God, to humble Himself even to the point of death, and to triumph over the wicked law of Satan are clearly demonstrated before the eyes of humankind. It is within God's power to be brought low and to be lifted up, to be brought to the deepest depths of suffering and raised in glory forever; to punish humankind and to reconcile them to God; to be humbled and exalted; to release humankind from their sin which leads to death by dying sinless on their behalf; to lay down the life of His only Son in order to ransom the lives of His enemies. These are the truths that first trouble and confuse us because they transcend us. They free us from our trouble and confusion when we submit to their truthfulness. But to the one who believes slavery is freedom, free people will always appear to be slaves.

Is the evidence of the cross a hopeless contradiction, another random event in a universal history of utter chaos and confusion? Was it simply a story created to pacify humankind and keep them in submission to religion? Or does it point to the purpose and authority of God, whose character and abilities are beyond our comprehension? Does it paint a picture of the result of total madness or love? The apostle Paul answered these questions aptly, "But we preach Christ crucified: a stumbling block to Jews and foolishness to Gentiles" (1 Corinthians 1:23). By its nature, the cross never became more or less culturally neutral, socially relevant, or rational—except to those who ignore its meaning so that they may remain unaffected by it as they travel along the wide road. The truth of the Gospel is such *good* news that it will continue to offend humans, as long as the deceptive desires of their heart are *evil* continually (Jeremiah 17:9; Genesis 6:5). Yet God will always offer freedom to those who are able to perceive and understand, to come as helpless children who know that human reason alone is never enough. The Gospel still stands as a rock of offense to those who hear it, and the cornerstone of freedom to those who perceive it by the help of God.

GK Chesterton said it well, "The cross opens its arms to the four winds; it is a signpost to free travelers." Truly the cross stands at once within the world and apart from the pattern of the world—a pattern that has only held humankind in bondage. The cross is the intersection of heaven and earth, the history of humankind and the character of God. It is the culmination of the sin of humankind from beginning to end and the physical proof that there is both freedom from it and punishment for it. Freedom begins at the end of this life. History did not stop at Calvary; it continued onward. But the cross has always been and will always be present in history's past and future. Christ is always in the mind of humans, either as nothing or as everything. He will always be central. He will never be neutral. No matter how popular it is in the culture, shrugging at salvation is a dangerous game.

HE ROLLED BACK THE STONE

The external evidence of Jesus'
resurrection confirms the truth we have
received via God's written word.

—Gary Habermas

THERE IS A DESTINATION FOR each person. Either we go to heaven, to hell, to the grave, to nirvana, are reincarnated, or something else. Everybody has a destination narrative that correlates with their worldview, even if it rests dormant in their unconscious. Such a narrative may end in hope or hopelessness. Ceasing to exist altogether is itself a destination story of sorts, even if the destination is nothing more than physical decomposition. Every person holds true to one story or another, even if they do not think very much about mortality. Christ didn't teach a different type of destination, but demonstrated one—and He was the only one to do so. In His resurrection, He showed true destination. As the author of our origin, He was the only one with the *authority* to likewise author our destination.

Recognizing God's authority and our subsequent lack of authority over our own destination, aside from the narratives we create to make sense of death, makes the resurrection perpetually difficult to believe in because it altogether eliminates our own agency in the matter. It proves all our theories wrong, and it proves God right. Moreover, it shows that Christ is the only one we can fully trust the end of our lives to. Christ was raised from death by God. Humans cannot be raised without God, no matter how much they say they can. Christ's resurrection troubles those who want total control over their destination. Not only that, but now they must learn even to doubt death, the only thing in this life that they learned they can be certain of. The resurrection of Jesus didn't only trouble the skeptics and critics; it confused even those closest to Him, those who had witnessed all His authority and divinity up to that point. Believers in the resurrection today are no less prone to be confused by it, and to lack even the most elementary understanding of it. To the degree that one understands the cross, one grows in knowledge of the cost of forgiveness. To the degree that one understands the resurrection, one grows more abundantly in a *living* hope, a hope that is not based on myth or philosophy but on history and reality. The cross tells the story of the reconciliation of God and humanity through the death of Christ. The resurrection tells of the reconciliation of God and humanity through the life of Christ. It points to a specific eternity which has been promised and modeled, not a hypothesized eternity.

At the time of Jesus, many did not believe in bodily resurrection, and today, much of the same thinking surrounds the apparent finality of death. The body and life on earth are seen by some as a temporary test run. The physical body can be viewed even as carnal or evil, and the shedding of the body at the end of life can be seen as a good thing. The spirit is set free from its bodily bondage once and for all to travel at light speed through the cosmos. Many take the opposite position, that this life in this body is all we have. When the heart stops beating and brain stops churning, there is nothing more. Which position is the correct one? Can both be right, or wrong? The bodily resurrection of Jesus was not just a deviation from the sequence of normal death. It proved death rather to be the abnormality, even though so far it happens to everyone. When we saw this, we caught a glimpse of the only destination story that was not man-made.

There is no physical abandonment or absence of spirit. Instead, God demonstrates in raising His Son *physically* by the power of His *spirit* (since God is spirit) that the belief in Christ's bodily resurrection includes both the fullness of body (bodily immortality) and the fullness of spirit (unity with God's spirit). Christ's resurrection does not submit to either human extremes. It is therefore not reductive. It illustrates an unimaginable destination, precisely because it was not imagined, but demonstrated. God performed Christ's resurrection. He did not write us a twelve-step program to achieve it.

In the earliest church after Jesus's death and resurrection, the resurrection was central. In fact, most of the Apostle Paul's teachings concerning Jesus were primarily focused on His death and resurrection, not His other miracles or the content of His teachings. Paul considered Christ's resurrection to be the most important affirmation of His deity. The resurrection, therefore, could not have been an account that arose in mystical writings many years after Jesus's life on earth. Neither was it a take it or leave it part of Christian doctrine. It was universal in the earliest church and uncontested within its orthodox beliefs, and it was central to the momentum and survival of the faith to this day. As stated, it was referred to many times in the writings of Paul and other apostles, and its earliest origins of verbal circulation can be historically traced back most likely to within one to a few years after the historical resurrection. An honest examination of the early church's belief in Christ's resurrection reminds us of two things: if this event was faked, it would have been relatively easy to debunk at the time and its legend would be quelled; and it was impossible even for the contemporary enemies of the Way to discredit the resurrection, although at least one attempt was made to do exactly this (Matthew 28). Even the Jewish officials caused an uproar about guarding the tomb after Jesus's death to make sure His followers wouldn't steal His body in order to perform a hoax. Likewise, those who heard the apostles' message would have been able to verify the accounts of the many eyewitnesses of the risen Christ, finding out if it was true for themselves (1 Corinthians 15). Paul's letter to the Corinthians reminds them that many eyewitnesses of the risen Christ were still living. Today, thousands of years after the event, we still hold in our hands the direct accounts from these earliest sources, which were reliant on, and in some cases written by firsthand eyewitnesses to Jesus and His resurrection. If this were not the case, and if the resurrection was a hoax then, it still would be easy to demystify today. Yet those who set out on an honest errand to adequately discredit the resurrection continue to come up short, often ending up as believers themselves. There are many reasons to trust the validity of the resurrection historically and its scriptural account. But here we will talk about what the resurrection means for us today and how it differs from the destinations of modernity.

Both aspects of the modern beliefs surrounding end of life, be they natural or ethereal, are as exclusive as Christianity, which both aspects criticize for its exclusivity. The modern extremes are exclusive in their mandatory inclusiveness, as one who disagrees with these man-made destination theories are often ridiculed for either believing that there is something more or nothing more. For example, if every person dies and is buried in the ground and there is nothing more, as atheism assures us is true, nobody by nature can be excluded from this natural process—thus anyone who disagrees with this hypothesis by nature is *excluded* from knowledge of the truth. If every person's spirit upon death is released and free to float forever around the universe, as may be supposed by the amalgam of new spirituality, nobody by nature is *excluded* from this supernatural process either. Likewise, all who disagree with this hypothesis are excluded from knowledge of its truth. The result is an unavoidable predetermined exclusion from either natural or supernatural, depending on the mood of the one you're disagreeing with. There are two opposing views on death that by their very claims to include everyone, exclude anyone who doubt those claims. Furthermore, in either case everyone is excluded entirely from one or the other—body or spirit—and subsequently barred in a prison of material decay or total ghostliness.

There is also a lack of choice in the matter as to which destination one is allowed to participate in. Every spirit must be either universally separated from body or entirely snuffed out, and if one or the other is the correct interpretation, everyone on the other side of the prevailing belief is barred from their intended destination.

Believing in the bodily resurrection of Jesus troubles both these extremes. This is challenging for many to believe, largely because so far it has only happened to one person, but if that one person indeed held a higher authority when he told us the truth about our destination, *and then demonstrated this truth for us to see*, shouldn't we hold that truth at a higher standard than our own biased guess as to what happens? The Bible tells us that the resurrection is a hope that grows through faith in Christ, not an indiscriminate theory that "includes" everyone via intellectual coercion. It is therefore the only explanation that differs from man-made destinations. Once again, our daily reality of having the freedom of choice in where we get to turn and walk is most aptly reflected in the Christian paradigm.

The trouble for so many with the resurrection is that so far it is so exclusive that it has only included one. However, if one believes the resurrection to be true, though there have not been others who have been glorified after death in the same way as Jesus, one can still observe the sheer mass of God's promise in a historical event—that through faith, like Jesus, we too *may* participate in His resurrection. Why would this isolated, ancient case study be enough to outweigh all the other afterlife theories that prevail within our culture? Because there is multifaceted evidence of the resurrection. God indeed raised Jesus from the dead. Therefore, God is real, and Jesus is who He said He was. What He says triumphs over what we say. The biblical account holds divine authority, and so do Jesus's teachings. If God promised the same type of resurrection for His children, then based on His previously demonstrated power and authority, one should consider a physical resurrection as the weightier truth, even though so far it only has happened to one person.

The resurrection is exclusive, this cannot be denied. One can only participate in it by knowing the one to whom it has been given. It is not a final inclusion of all the various precepts and worldviews, but the dominant and liberating assertion of one man's unquestionable authority over all the constants in the world which currently hold authority over humanity, primarily sin and death. It is by Jesus's victory over sin through submission to His Father that He was also given power over death and was able to make death itself submit to Him. The resurrection also acknowledges the unknown laws of the afterlife without dismissing the known laws of this life. It is the true bridge between this world and the next. But this bridge can only be understood in Christ, by believing He is the unique Son of God. Christ's life was never forgotten because it was never even lost. God did not build this world or us to be forgotten either. If God fulfilled His promise of salvation to us through His Son, would it be wise to ignore this promise? Can we really expect God to force one to partake in the salvation they've chosen to reject? God chooses those who choose Christ for a destination too wonderful for us to fully comprehend. There is an equal and opposite reaction of destination in the case of rejection. Christ told the story. God has provided human beings with the free will to choose a life that is either for Him or against Him. He is gracious enough to allow us to follow the path that we choose, regardless of the repercussions.

The glory of the resurrection ought to give a hope that is not in vain to all men and women, for it shatters the myth of hopelessness and death. But humans, as free agents, may choose to believe either in truth or myth. The truth, although rarer, cannot be shaken and has proven to be eternal, while the myth most certainly will die along with death itself.

IN THE BEGINNING
WAS THE WORD

The general theory of relativity, on its own,
cannot explain these features or answer
these questions because of its prediction
that the universe started off with infinite
density at the big bang singularity.

—Stephen Hawking

THERE IS A LOT THAT goes into a story, even apart from its
meaning and content. A story, or series of stories is made up of many
individual components such as letters, words, sentences, paragraphs,
and chapters, each one consisting of smaller and smaller fragments,
down to the lines and curves that form each letter. The resulting story
includes all of these divisible elements, but none of these elements
could exist within their higher purpose as part of the story without
the author who organizes the story.

Effective stories are specific. They are ordered in a specific
way for a specific purpose by a specific person. As we learned in
grade school, a successful story needs to be more than the various
structures and sounds that it consists of, as a person is more than the
sum of their parts. Story needs purpose. There is a moral to every
story, or at least there ought to be. The Bible is a unique story in

that it is simultaneously the most loved, most hated, most quoted, and best-selling story in the known universe. It sells well because it contains the epitome of "the moral to the story" and because of the controversy that arises out of the implication of this moral. It is often rejected because it is seen as lacking authorial coherence as well as more modernized ideals of morality—of course these criticisms make more sense under the preconditions that accompany naturalism. The Bible has a lot to say and makes a lot of sobering claims which ought to be deeply considered and to change our lives if they are true. There are therefore a lot of attacks which are meant to counter the urgency and authority of scripture, and generations of eloquent defenses still stand to counter those attacks. It is alternatively recognized and to some degree respected as having literary or moral value even to those who do not fully believe the validity of its message, even though it is not designed to do this. The red letters are often the most quoted, and most people still try to live by the golden rule, even if they deny this is what they're aspiring to day to day. Being a person of eternal cultural influence, Christ's must be a story with a pretty good moral attached, or at least one that comes into contact with many things that are both common and uncommon to humanity.

Every good story has a moral *only if* that moral makes a good point, for a meandering series of words is more likely to confuse and frustrate the reader than edify them. The same rule may be applied to the life of a person. What is the moral to the story of your life, or mine? A good life only has a good story if it has a point; "The integrity of the upright guides them, but the unfaithful are destroyed by their duplicity" (Proverbs 11:3). Notice that the first person is guided by their integrity and their character, whereas the latter is led to destruction by duplicity, or deception. Which person do the elements of chaos belong to? Of structure and order?

There is a point to the story of our lives, but we don't write this point, any more than words create their own meaning on a page. The point of life is there at the beginning, and is there all the way until the end, but it merits integrity or uprightness to understand that it is there, and an elaborate lie to undermine such a mundane fact. It is the essence of someone—their inherent, God-given value and design. This value is the first word at conception and the last period upon our last breath. The value of life can be heeded or rejected just like the Word of God. The point of a book likewise is its essence, which is needed for it to persevere towards its moral word by word, sentence by sentence. Moreover, the moral of our lives may be seen as the intent given by the one who has given our essence to us. A story's essence tells its story, and is infused by its author. Deviating from the plot line makes it unreadable—the moral never emerges as both story and author are denied.

Sometimes the point we set out to make at the beginning of a story is forgotten by the end. We ask ourselves either, "What was my point?" or much worse, "What is the point?" and crumple up the paper to throw in the trash. Such a meandering story was unlikely to captivate anyone. A meaningless life, no matter how grandiose the actions found within, is similarly likely to leave one feeling empty, like there is no point, and often despairing of life itself.

From the moment the author's pen hits the paper, the burden is on them to make their point. The Bible is either loved or hated because it either makes a very good point or invariably fails to arrive at one. It must be viewed intellectually in one of these two ways—as holding or withholding the key to the meaning of life itself.

When the essence of a story or its author is extracted, the cohesiveness of that story ceases to exist (1 Corinthians 15:14). It is no longer consistent, the sequences break down into fragmented and unintelligible parts, and the story has no more direction or thrust. Even postmodern stories that sought to rid themselves of any cohesion whatsoever set out to make the point of lacking any point. More often than not, they succeed in their goal of not making any perceivable point, aside from what the individual reader may project. Whatever any story ends up meaning in the end, it arose as a construct and a reflection of the mind of the writer—whether they sought to demolish something that had meaning from the beginning or to build something meaningful, even out of the end.

Every story would fail to arrive at its destination without the intent of its author. The best stories are the ones where the author writes aspects of themselves into the fabric of the text. How else do they make their stories realistic, relatable, and readable? There is a conspiracy theory that says the writings of Shakespeare are inauthentic. There have been many more who look at the writings of God in the same way, putting much more at stake in such an assumption. To remove Shakespeare from his own plays and poems would degrade their value and authenticity, as well as dilute our knowledge of Shakespeare. The same attempt to strip God of scriptural authorship seems to rob scripture of its meaning, which includes its basic logic. If God is also the author of creation and life itself, "as the story goes," one may want to honestly weigh the possible consequences of removing God from one's life completely— as secular scholars have pulled Him out of the pages of scripture. Frankly, neither of these stories are meant to be read in such a way.

The design of the pages of the good book, and the pages that may be written about our days imply a hands on God, who doesn't allow any reasoning which includes Him only as a partial author. Thus reading the Bible or reading our lives somewhere on a spectrum ranging from godless to God-fearing is unreasonable by nature of reason. Understanding the authority of God as shown in scripture and coming to terms with the *historical* Jesus ought to deeply impact our interpretation of the various stories we face, and the points they are trying to make.

Interpretations of the Bible range from utterly meaningless to completely inerrant. Where one falls on this spectrum depends on how much authorship, agency, and intent they believe God to have. The essence of the Bible illustrates the nature of God. If God has zero authorship, the Bible has no truthful essence, a principle implicit in its design. On the other hand, if God has ultimate authorship, then the Bible contains the answers for life's ultimate meaning, but only through God. There can of course be a human argument for middle ground on this spectrum, but an impartial evaluation of the Bible will rationally lead to a conclusion on one or the other extreme concerning the matter of authorship. If partial divine authorship is the case, scripture would have some meaning and some value in reflecting God's nature, but finding exactly where and when the divinity is apparent or absent in the scriptures would be vague and unclear, requiring more subjective interpretations. One could not read the Word without wondering what to trust and what not to, placing certain emphasis on certain texts while ignoring others altogether for the sake of convenience. Affirming the authorship only of some scripture inevitably dilutes the authority of all scripture.

On the other hand, the divine authority of scripture would give credit to all of it, without forgetting that the authors God used were human individuals with differing designs and relationships with God. God promises His Word will outlive the universe. The distinction between doubting and believing things like this becomes increasingly clear when the immutable reality of the one who said these things is taken into account. Certainly, if there is a God who created and sustains everything to this day, it would be foolish to presume that He couldn't communicate one story and sustain its message throughout the ages.

Many people vary in how they see the Bible. Some see it as totally infallible. Others see it as completely untrustworthy. But most, quite honestly, do not actually see it in either of these extremes; they only lean further to one side than the other. As a Christian, I lean increasingly toward total biblical infallibility, but there is still much within it that I struggle to understand, believe, or agree with. Meanwhile, those who claim to reject the Bible completely cannot realistically claim to completely disbelieve or disagree with all of it any more than one can claim to understand all of it. They cannot completely disbelieve it because it has mounting credibility both in provable historical and empirical content and it speaks to many conditions that are universal and undeniable to humanity.

More than that, critics cannot completely refute what they cannot understand, and they cannot understand anything that has been encrypted. The Bible by design is meant to be understood with the element of faith. One cannot completely understand the Word without faith because faith in the Word was intended by the author to be the interpretive key for the Word. Those who do not have faith are therefore unable to engage with the Word in the way it was intended to be understood by its author, even if those with such a key are still imperfect in understanding.

Put simply, a bodybuilder may struggle to understand biochemistry, and a biochemist may struggle to bench press 350 pounds. The critic cannot understand faith any more than the person of faith can understand total doubt. The mundane fact remains, a subject cannot be understood even in its most elementary form without some level of engagement. A story cannot be listened to without at some point hearing the voice and mind of its creator. The two are inseparable. Therefore, by engaging with any given text one is also engaging at some level with the intent of its author. One will come across the tone of the author of scripture, for God's intent is displayed in the content of His Word—and that intent is knowledge of Him. The expression of the author will make its impression on the reader as long as the reader reads with an open mind. Without this relationship between the reader and the author, the story is lost, along with its point and the moral of the story. To examine scripture impartially and critically ultimately will result in stumbling across its true author. If this author is divine and created everything, including space and time, His writings will pervade all things. There can be nothing in nature that remains hidden from His words, because His words created nature.

Either the Bible stands alone, towering over every human story we know, or it melts into the genre of fantasy as its truth is undermined. Without God, the Bible becomes an empty tomb, another purely natural literary phenomenon that has a beginning, a middle, and an end—a man-made moral rooted in deception. Its effects become another product of psychological evolution, with nothing at its core but survival of the fittest, just like everything else. The nagging trouble is that everyone who actually looks at the Bible can't help but see *something*. They might like what they see, they might not. But they cannot presume that, just like everything else, it scuttled out of the primordial literary pond. Its pages claim to hold true knowledge of the source of everything, and He who is the "One God and Father of all, who is over all and through all and in all" (Ephesians 4:6). If there is a point to the Bible, it's that its author is God.

BRIDGING THE GAP

Jesus answered, "I am the way
and the truth and the life.
No one comes to the Father except through me."

—John 14:6

I REALIZE THAT COMING TO FAITH can seem impossibly hard for many reasons. Belief can seem like an incredibly far distance to travel in an age when Christianity appears to be receding quicker than ever from all areas of life. This book is meant to be a reminder and an encouragement concerning the trustworthiness of the faith in the midst of its cultural recession.

The Christian way of seeing the world still rests in total faith that God created the universe and everything in it, and moreover that He did not step away; the other viewpoint rests in total quantifiable rationality—if it cannot be seen, it cannot be. The chasm between faith and modernity is eternally widening. It stretches between worlds and ways, and across paradigms and patterns. Standing on one side and looking across at the other is enough to terrify, but coming to terms with the presence of the chasm answers many questions. For the fact remains that every one of us will spend our lives on one side of it or the other, and our lives will eventually come to an end no matter which side we're on. There is no denying death no matter how much our actions and attitudes fly in the face of it.

Death does not discriminate between races, genders, or classes. It grants us all equality under its law. It will not very much care what our opinions were about it, and it will almost always come more suddenly than we'd like it to. As long as it is called "today," we live perpetually under its threat. Death is certainly the most troubling part of nature because it is at once so unnatural and universal. When it comes, it is hard to see because we cannot see it coming. This is death's greatest trick. The Bible rightly tells us that the gap between the temporary and the eternal cannot always be seen but *will* always be found, no matter what temporary things we cling to in this life. When death finds us, we will find God awaiting an answer, even if we've chosen to ignore Him. It is not we who get to question Him. We've done that all our lives. Now it's His turn.

The book of Proverbs says, "There is a way that seems right to a man, but in the end it leads to death" (Proverbs 14:12). God brought about our beginning. He can bring about our end. As our creator and sustainer, He has the right to do this. At our end, all humanity's theories about religion, being and self will become obsolete in the presence of the truth. They will melt away before Him. At that point, *the only important thing in our lives* will be the way in which we responded to God. Did we see Him in His truth or through the lens of the lies of the world, the enemy, and our own hearts? At that time, God will no longer be an optional idea to be accepted or brushed off, but a reality more present than the physical universe which now lies behind us. Are you ready for that day? Everything you built your life around apart from God, whether it was family, finance, friends or folly, will crumble like leaves and blow away in the wind. All things apart from Him will be made known as shadows, dust and ashes. We can spend our whole lives trying to make an educated guess, or we can make the best *guess*, which God has assured us is certain. The certainty is in His Son.

Jesus and the prophets before Him were able to see the yawning chasm that lies open between God and those who rebel against Him. "With cunning they conspire against your people; they plot against

THE BEST GUESS

those you cherish" (Psalm 83:2). Before Jesus came, salvation came to the Hebrews. Those regulations in all their complexities were only a shadow of what was to come; "Because it is impossible for the blood of bulls and goats to take away sins" (Hebrews 10:4). Throughout this time, God patiently waited and watched for true faith among His followers, and even among outsiders. He does the same today. Only now, we see that Jesus has made the old way obsolete, just like He has made the old self obsolete. For who we are in our sins is only a shadow of what is to come. *Today*, He calls us to sojourn into the new world with Him. Abraham believed in the promise, and it was credited to him as righteousness. So can we trust in the promise God has given us. God's promises cannot be seen or examined in a test tube any more than He can, but they ought to be thoughtfully considered, and once considered they ought to be faced, feared, respected, and hoped for. It is only by His Word and His promises that we walk the earth we walk and breathe the air we breathe. Every person on earth has been given this first gift of life. Everyone faces the choice to worship either the gift or its giver. If we worship the gift, we end up worshipping ourselves as the ones worthy of the gift. It is the choice of who we worship that is the seed for all the controversy in this book. It is this choice that splits apart paradigms and therefore comes like a sword between people (Matthew 10:34).

The sword is God's Word. I realize that to many, it may seem like a contradiction that Jesus is called the Prince of Peace yet assures the world that He has come to divide it. This is quite an unconventional way to build a bridge across the yawning chasm long seen by the prophets. When one thinks of a sword, they do not often think of peace, but often, using the sword is the only way to bring peace. If the Allies only talked about peace during World War Two and hid in their homes, allowing the Axis powers to continue their ruthless campaign, we would live in a very different world today. The sword of the Bible and the swords of the world paradoxically become symbols of both death and peace. But Christ was not speaking about the sword of the world or of the flesh, but of the Spirit. The sword of the Spirit brings peace to the lives of men and women by dividing the good from the evil within us and judging the thoughts and intents of our hearts with a truth higher than our own—indeed much higher. Good and evil, which were blended in our pursuit of their knowledge, can only be distinguished by Christ, not by our own interpretation.

Christ's need for the sword of the Spirit shows that faith in Christ must come by means of death of one kind to avoid death of another. "Whoever finds his life will lose it, and whoever loses his life for my sake will find it" (Matthew 10:39). Jesus built the bridge to life by showing us His life, which was true life, and ultimately laying it down for us that we may find it. His example was not simply as a wise teacher with a lot of clever things to say. He was God on earth. He taught humans how to find the narrow way to true life. His mission and His identity were sewn into His DNA. Humankind must see that true life in the Son can be shared only by participating in His death so that we may by the power of God also participate in His resurrection. This becomes the new *fact* of life. It is one that has been made available only to be listened to with reverence or sneered at in disbelief—the option of indifference or neutrality is not left open to rational beings.

When Jesus taught that He is the bread of life, and that humankind must eat His flesh and drink His blood to have life, it scattered the crowds that followed Him. It greatly troubled and angered His hearers. It still does. No matter how much more wide open we think this chasm between Christ and the pattern of this world lies today, it was the same then. No matter how wide people thought the chasm was then, it is no narrower now. The distinction between knowledges has never changed. We are as we have always been, stuck beneath the world's biggest question mark, and there is only one way to move forward (John 1:12).

AFTERWORD

Addressing the Elephant in the Room

I was reminded of a maxim this week: "We all have a 'piece of the elephant'." What this maxim is referring to is an old philosophical precept about the fallibility of truth claims. Suppose you and I had never heard of an elephant before and both of us were taken into a dark room wherein an elephant stood (hopefully not an elephant in musth). The maxim declares that you and I, blindly groping throughout the dark room, may likely stumble onto different parts of the elephant's body, say the trunk or tail. Grabbing hold of the trunk, you tell me what you learn about elephants, that they are large, round, bendable, and wiggly—or however you may better describe an elephant's trunk than me. I disagree, though. I say that an elephant is more like the part of the body that I have my hand on—the tail.

The broader point of this analogy is to say that we all grope around similarly through this world, and truth claims in general or religion in particular are like the elephant in the room. As a Christian, I have a hold of a leg, a Buddhist has a hold of the ear, a Hindu the trunk, an atheist the tail, and so on.

It is a clever adage, but ultimately self-defeating in its logic—as more affluent thinkers than myself have discovered. Quite simply, claiming there are no truth claims is itself a truth claim and therefore redundant, just like claiming "everyone has a piece of the elephant" is a maxim that was obviously told by a person who had superior knowledge about elephants than those who grope around the room. Unfortunately for whoever cleverly coined the adage, the counterargument to the adage became much more interesting than the adage itself. There are a number of reasons for this.

First, the adage is often not only an adage, but a synopsis of a pluralistic worldview which may be invoked for any number of reasons; respecting others' opinions, maintaining a number of open spiritual options, or attempting to undermine someone else's truth claim, for example. The elephant in the room argument, which as we've seen rests on a faulty presupposition, is indeed often a microcosm of a much larger argument, which is worldview. Therefore the counterargument to this maxim is often brushed to the side regardless of its effectiveness.

Second, the "higher" truth claim against truth claims is not held exclusively by the person who invented the elephant in a dark room metaphor, but extends to anyone who uses the argument or thinks it's true. If I am arguing with somebody and need to invoke the elephant in a dark room metaphor, it means inherently that I see their view as more simplistic than my own. Even though I can temporarily concede to being one of the volunteers in the dark room, I am actually simultaneously the knower and teller of the metaphor—even though I have my hand on the leg or the ear or the tail, I was also the one who turned off the lights and started the experiment, as it were. Therefore, those who relate the metaphor, even as the inventor of the metaphor did, are only pretending to be an impartial observer of the elephant. Actually they believe themselves to be the only expert on elephants present in the room. The author and reciter of the metaphor become one.

Third, the elephant metaphor rests on the assumption that the dark room is the only world available. There is no leaving the room and googling information about elephants. The people in the experiment are therefore restricted to the one piece of the elephant that they can touch. Somehow they even become stagnant *within the very room* and are not permitted to move about from one part of the elephant to another in order to get the bigger picture about elephants. Of course the metaphor deals with a lofty hypothetical in this sense (where even if you are, say, touching the elephant's tail, you aren't even allowed to move your hand over six inches to the side in order to touch the animal's buttocks. I know, "cheeky," right?). This hypothetical is grossly restrictive in what it allows the participants to do, if we assume "participation in the dark room experiment" to be analogous to "humanity's search for ultimate truth and meaning," or something of the like. Before such an experiment was conducted, one would likely presume that the person conducting it, who had full knowledge of elephants beforehand, held a half hour seminar in another room, insisting on a number of rules for the participants to follow so that the results of the experiment would be desirable— that the people learn absolutely nothing more about elephants than they ought to learn. The whole thing smacks of determinism, as the results of the elephant in the dark room experiment are already predetermined by the conductor of the experiment. The metaphor assumes that no further truth about elephants can be known apart from the unlikely parameters of the metaphor.

The broader point of this elephantine maxim is meant to discredit whichever person the conductor sees as actually being the conductor by making a truth claim about elephants. Take Christianity for example, as this maxim is usually a response to the exclusive claims of Christianity. The Christian is seen as the person who wrongly believes himself to understand the bigger picture. However, by reducing the Christian's claim of "absolute knowledge" to a partial knowledge which can be no more or less than another's partial knowledge, the vacuum of "absolute knower" must be filled—and is presumably filled by the very person that says they've undermined the Christian's argument *by arguing that there is no identifiable basis to argue on.*

My last point on the matter is this: Christians do not claim to be the only ones who know what elephants look like. We simply claim that there is an elephant, and when conducting the elephant experiment we say that people ought to be allowed to move around the elephant *freely* and touch different parts of it, as well as communicate with the others in the room about what they've discovered, something the other conductor did not allow for. If we have a "truth claim," it is only that there is an abundant availability of resources on the subject of elephants, even if we are unlikely to encounter one anywhere but in a dark room, that is until we are permitted to leave the room.

Moreover, our "truth claim" is not our truth claim at all, but someone else's—therefore, our opinion on the matter holds no weight apart from the one who we know has the power to turn the lights on and off. This is why, even if the elephant maxim is correct, which it isn't, the resurrection of Christ overturns its basic conclusion.

ABOUT THE AUTHOR

Sam Wittke is an aspiring writer who has been following Jesus for four years. He loves to encourage people that there is always hope when life gets tough and the usual answers aren't cutting it.

Printed in the United States
by Baker & Taylor Publisher Services